Oxford University Press 19

Streets Ahead
Teacher's Book 2

Maggie Murray & Norland Smith

Overview

	SOAP	GRAMMAR	LANGUAGE AREA
1	*On the air* Sylvia interviews Sir Robert Firth, Minister for the Environment.	Present perfect Present perfect with *already, yet*, and *just* Present perfect and past simple	Interviewing The environment Traffic
2	*In the dark* Poppy and Max's car breaks down on a lonely country road.	*will/won't* *will* or *going to*? Comparative adjectives	Making comparisons Giving directions Asking favours
3	*An Englishman's home* Tom and Archie find the Longthorpe treasure.	*have/has to* *don't/doesn't have to* *should/shouldn't* Present perfect with *for/since, ever/never*	Doing up houses Obligation; Advice; Suggestions Money
4	*The inside track* Rita goes running, and Hank wants to give up his law studies.	Adverbs of manner (*-ly*) Question tags *want(s) to do/want(s) somebody to do* Present perfect with *for/since*	Agreeing: Confirming information Studies Sport
5	*Food for thought* Toby and Anna talk about the future.	First conditional Reflexive verbs and pronouns	Food and restaurants Talking about jobs
6	*Olympic hurdle* Rita is in big trouble. Max promises to help.	Defining and non-defining relative clauses *one/ones* *used to* Reported speech 1	Asking for things in shops Sport; Medicine; Illness Talking about change
7	*All the world's a stage* Suzi auditions for a part in a play at the National Youth Theatre.	Reported speech 2 *when* clauses	Talking about ambitions Talking about what you have heard Giving instructions
8	*Things that go bump in the night* Toby and Max help Archie with his plans to save the castle. There are strange noises after dark.	First conditional Second conditional Superlative adjectives	Talking about hypothetical situations Holiday towns; Buildings
9	*Wedding bells* Anna is late! Everybody waits outside the Registry Office.	Past continuous *when/until* clauses *must/mustn't* *too . . ./not . . . enough*	Weddings Describing people; Personalities
10	*Stormy weather* A storm hits the Irish Sea during the Fastnet race. Max, Toby, and Tom are in danger.	Passive sentences Conjunctions of time Clauses as noun phrases	Describing and comparing boats Getting things done The weather
Epilogue	*All's Well that Ends Well* Max and Poppy have a party. There is much to celebrate.		

PRONUNCIATION	READING	LISTENING	OPTIONS
Word stress Weak forms /ə/	Sylvia's story (memos)	Radio news headlines	Grammar/Numbers/Grammar and vocabulary/Small talk/Time
Sentence stress /ɔː/ /ʊə/ /ɑː/	Ashbourne, Derbyshire	Travel news	Vocabulary/Translation/Grammar/Travelling 1/Travelling 2/Further practice
Word stress Past tense /t/ /d/ /ɪd/	Hide-and-seek A narrow escape A newspaper story	A narrow escape	Listening/Your home/Small talk/Measurements/Reading for information/Dates
Sentence stress /ə/ /æ/ /ɑː/ /ɔ/ /eɪ/ Rhyming words	Antarctic expedition Hank's CV	Antarctic expedition	Grammar/Puzzle/Further practice/Vocabulary/Enrichment/Listening
Word stress Sentence stress /iː/ /e/ /ɜː/ /ɪə/	Desmond's day Restaurant advertisements	Two interviews	Small talk/Enrichment/Out and about/Puzzle/Vocabulary/Personal life
Word stress Stress and intonation Rhyming words	Drugs and sport	My room	Grammar/Further practice/Small talk/Time
Sentence stress /s/ /z/ /ʃ/ Intonation	Interviews and auditions	Suzi's audition	About the house/Discussion/Vocabulary/Grammar/Messages/Comments/Enrichment
Word stress Stress and intonation /ɪ/	Christmas meeting	Leisure park	Enrichment/Revision/Vocabulary/Reading for information/Reading/Small talk
Sentence stress Rhyming words Intonation	Murder at Fenley End House	Murder at Fenley End House Do you sail?	Social idioms/Language/Further practice/Enrichment/Small talk/Revision
Word stress /ɔː/ /ɜː/ /əʊ/ /eɪ/ Reading phonetic script	Surviving the storm Lost at sea	What happened to *Lion*?	Quantities/Vocabulary/Small talk/Further practice

Introduction

1 WHO THE COURSE IS FOR

Learners and their interests

Streets Ahead 2 is a course for adults and young adults at pre-intermediate level. Many of them are already at work or moving towards a career, and their interests generally centre on work, family, and leisure. All these sources have been taken into account in the planning of the course, and in the decision to base it on a 'soap' – an ongoing, loosely connected series of episodes in which a small group of characters reappear.

The mother tongue

It is assumed that most of the teachers using the course will be teaching monolingual groups of students living in the same place. For this reason, we have provided exercises such as translation and preparatory work in the mother tongue.

Each exercise has the following symbols:
- o   (L1 – mother tongue)
- ●   (L2 – English)
- o ● (L1 and/or L2)

The familiar and the new

In recent years, there has been a welcome injection of more communicative approaches into language teaching. These approaches allow students to spend more classroom time *using* the language rather than *learning about* the language. However, for older students, learning about language – particularly grammar – is a familiar and reassuring activity. This course therefore includes familiar activities of this sort at the early stages, and becomes more function- and skills-centred as the course progresses. This is in line with the philosophy of many modern syllabuses, which move from a mainly grammatical orientation to a more functional/skills-centred one.

2 HOW THE COURSE IS DESIGNED

General principles

The material is designed to indicate clearly to teachers and students the purpose of each exercise or task. We have tried to provide a wide variety of exercises and classroom activities, giving opportunities for individual work in the classroom or at home.

We have deliberately limited the amount of material on a page, in order to provide motivation for students, who turn the pages quickly and have a feeling of progress, and reassurance for teachers, who can see that the material is manageable in the time available.

Overview of the sections

The units of the Student's Book are divided into a number of sections, each with a different purpose.

Preview   This section introduces or revises the new language for the unit, and is designed as presentation rather than practice material.

The story   Each chapter of the story is an episode in a genuine 'soap', based on a developing plot and characters who also appear in some of the exercises. The language is colloquial and naturalistic, containing examples of the target structures and vocabulary. It also provides a thematic focal point for each unit.

Performance   This consists of seven sections on:

Comprehension   These exercises provide a rapid review of the story. They can be done as pair work, or more often, individually and then checked in pairs.

Practice   This section reinforces the new language (grammatical and functional) in the story.

Pronunciation   Student's Book 2 concentrates on three aspects of pronunciation:

1 Practice of the phonetic symbols used to represent English speech. The transcriptions are those of the *Oxford Advanced Learner's Dictionary*.

2 Word stress. Correct stress is vital to successful communication in English. Try to give stress practice regularly, using your own lists of words.

3 Sentence stress. The connection between one sentence and another is often only clear if the main stress in the sentence falls in the right position. Again, this is an essential skill for successful communication.

With pronunciation skills, 'little and often' is the best way to practise. Do not spend too much time on these exercises, or go into too much detail.

Reading   At this stage, students read for a limited purpose (to obtain information, for example). They do not need to understand everything in the text. The texts are realistic, and written in a variety of styles such as students might come across in everyday life.

Further narrative texts (reading for pleasure) are included in the Workbook.

Listening   These are unseen listenings for the vital extra listening practice that is needed at this level. They are short, realistic, and usually conversational in tone.

Grammar Summary   Each teaching unit ends with a Grammar Summary which provides reference material for the student.

Options   The Options are a selection of different activities that expand on items from the main sections, or introduce interesting smaller items. The activities are generally short and fun to do. An approximate time indication is given, so that you can choose according to time available and your students' needs.

3   LEARNING VOCABULARY

Vocabulary can be a problem for teachers. Students do not learn vocabulary in the neat and orderly fashion prescribed in textbooks. They learn what interests them. *Streets Ahead* assumes a low active core vocabulary (the words are listed after each unit in the Workbook), and provides opportunities for students to expand their vocabulary in their own way, partly through exercises (where students find words connected with a topic area, or with their own work), partly through systematic vocabulary development in the Workbook. Try to spend some lesson time showing your students how to use the vocabulary sections of the Workbook on a regular basis and how to develop their ability to handle a

dictionary constructively. While it is up to them to expand their own vocabulary, regular use of these two tools will make it easier for them.

4   ADDITIONAL COMPONENTS

The Teacher's Book
This contains step-by-step notes on most of the exercises, the answers, and the tapescripts.

The Workbook
The *Streets Ahead* Workbook provides more than just practice exercises to reinforce the Student's Book. It is intended as an individual resource tool.

Grammar and practice exercises   Each unit has a number of standard workbook exercises. These are followed by a vocabulary review in which students not only check that they understand the core vocabulary, but also organize it into word families in the Vocabulary file for ease of reference.

Students transfer verbs to the Verb file, so that again they can refer to all the useful verb forms.

Each unit also contains a listening task, with the listening text recorded on the Student's Cassette.

Word play   This forms a separate section in the Workbook, with vocabulary puzzles which review the vocabulary encountered in the units.

Read it   This section provides a number of short prose reading texts. These are for reading for pleasure. There are formal questions, and students can retell the story in writing or in class.

Vocabulary file   This is to be used regularly at the end of each unit, so that students build up word families of useful vocabulary.

Verb file   This is also to be used regularly at the end of each unit.

The Cassettes
The 'soap' episodes and listening texts for exercises in the Student's Book are recorded on the Class Cassettes. Texts for the Workbook exercises and a slower version of the 'soap' episodes are on a separate Student's Cassette.

Introduction

- **Warm-up** Ask: *Look at the pictures of the people in the story. What do you remember about them?*

- **Presentation** Students look at the pictures and say: *That's* (Sylvia). *She's a* (radio reporter). *She's* (Toby's friend).

- **Practice** Students describe each of the characters, and should use English where possible. This is also an opportunity for students who used Book 1 to tell other students about the characters in the story.

- Students read *The story so far* to check what they have remembered. It also introduces the present perfect tense. If the students ask about it, tell them it is a new tense, which will be dealt with later. For the moment the students should look and try to understand how it is used.

1   Present perfect

a ○ ● **Explanation** This exercise introduces the present perfect and leads into the first episode of the story. It gives the students a lot of necessary listening practice with the new tense.

T.1.1 This scene takes place in an office at Central Radio News. Sylvia and her studio manager, Peter, are discussing an interview with Sir Robert Firth, a Member of Parliament. Sylvia's colleague, Jeff, telephoned earlier to say he had hurt his foot and could not come in to do the interview. Peter wants Sylvia to do the interview. The questions for the interview have already been prepared by Sir Robert. They are about his environment policies in the area. Sylvia agrees but is not happy that the questions do not include one about some land which is to be built

on. Sylvia has found out something important about this land and decides that, although Peter and Jeff promised not to ask questions about it, she has not promised anything, so *she* can ask Sir Robert.

- **Warm-up** The students read the introductory paragraph. Ask:

Who are the people talking?
Where are they?
What are they talking about?

Play the cassette and ask questions:

Why can't Jeff walk?
Who prepared the questions for the interview?
Who was supposed to do the interview?
Why was Sylvia not allowed to ask about the land?
Where did she find out her information about the land?
What did Sylvia find out?

b ○ ● **Presentation** Explain to the students that there is a new tense in the dialogues. Students identify it. Ask students to call out the first example of the present perfect tense that they can see in the passage: *Has Jeff arrived?*

○ ● **Practice** Students must find one example of each of the four forms of the present perfect tense. Make sure students know what a positive statement, etc., is, by doing the first few examples with them.

A **Positive statements**
Sir Robert has provided a list of questions. I've asked the Land Registry about this.
We've promised.
They've promised.

Negative statements
He hasn't included a question about the land.
I haven't promised.

Questions
Has Jeff arrived?
Have you looked at his notes?
What have you promised?

Short answers
No, he hasn't.
Yes, I have.

○ ● **Presentation**   Tell the students that the present perfect is used to link past events to the present, so it is a very good way of describing what has happened up to now. The students find further examples in *The story so far* and the introductory paragraph. Or ask them to try and *remember* any examples before they look.

○ ● **Practice**   Students work in pairs or alone and underline all the examples of the present perfect tense in the texts.

A   Poppy has married Max.
Tom has disappeared.
Suzi has recently left school.
Hank has been a law student.
Sylvia and Toby have returned from their holiday.
Jeff Coates has not arrived for an important interview with Member of Parliament Sir Robert Firth.
Peter has asked Sylvia to interview Sir Robert.
Sylvia has agreed to interview Sir Robert.

2   Past participles

○ ● **Presentation**   So far the students have been dealing with the regular past participles formed with *-ed* like the past simple. Here they are asked to recognize some irregular past participles. Read the first example: *She's taken the microphone.* Ask:

What is the past participle? What is the verb?
Can you remember the past simple? Do you think it is irregular or regular?

Students fill in the past simple and tick the 'irregular' box.

○ ● **Practice**   Students work in pairs to complete the table. They may need a dictionary for the past simple of verbs they cannot remember.

3   Present perfect and past simple

○ ● **Explanation**   There are many uses of the present perfect tense and it is sometimes difficult to choose between the present perfect and past simple tenses, but there are some rules to help students. For example, in English we never use the present perfect tense with a time phrase referring to a specific past point in time.

○ ● **Practice**   Go through the grammar explanation with the students to make sure that they understand it.

a ○ ● **Explanation**   This exercise allows the students to recognize the different uses of the present perfect and past simple tenses, without, at this stage, having to produce the new structure themselves.

○ ● **Warm-up**   Look at the example as a class. Ask two students to read the dialogue, one taking each part. Then discuss the two questions:

Which tense is used in each sentence?
Do we know exactly when the action happened?

In the first sentence, we know the action happened, but we don't know when exactly (hence the use of the present perfect tense). What is more important is that *they are here now*. In the second sentence, we know it was 'yesterday' (hence the use of the past simple), so 'yesterday' must be underlined.

○ ● **Practice**   Students work in small groups of three or four to study the three dialogues. They identify each verb and decide which tense it is in and whether it is used with a time phrase or not. Then they underline all the time phrases.

A   1 A present perfect
       B present perfect, past simple – *on Monday*, present perfect.
       A past simple – *last night*
     2 A present perfect
       B present perfect
       A past simple with *when*.
       B *on Monday morning* – past simple
     3 A present perfect
       B present perfect, past simple – *this morning*

● **Extension**   One or two pairs can act out each of the dialogues to practise the use of the present simple and present perfect tenses in everyday conversation.

b ○ ● Students work in pairs to translate the dialogues. Then, as a class, discuss any difference in the use of the tenses. In other languages it is often the case that all of these dialogues could be written in the past simple, as there would be no difference made here. If other languages have the same present perfect construction, i.e. *have* + past participle, it is often not used in the same way.

4 Vocabulary

a ○ ● **Explanation**   This exercise introduces vocabulary needed for the story.

○ ● **Warm-up**   Read the list of words carefully and talk about their meanings. Students may use a dictionary for words they are not sure of. Check that they can pronounce the words correctly.

○ ● **Practice**   Students find the words illustrated in the picture.

A	field house housing development stadium road bridge farmland sports centre traffic

b ○ ● Students work in pairs or small groups to put the words under the right headings in the table. Check the answers as a class.

A

People	Places	Town
taxpayer	stadium	bottleneck
owner	house	outskirts
minister	sports centre	house
	studio	housing development
		road
		sports centre
		traffic

Country	Government
region	planning permission
field	transport department
bridge	housing development
farmland	policy
environment	minister

On the Air

T.1.2 This is the scene of the interview. Sylvia has agreed to stand in for Jeff Coates, who is a more senior journalist. Sir Robert Firth is not very happy about the change but agrees to go ahead with the interview. Sir Robert Firth is Minister for the Environment as well as being the local MP. Sylvia questions Sir Robert about housing and road building in the Ledcombe area. Local people are not happy about losing their old bridge and having a housing development where they wanted leisure facilities to be built. Sylvia brings up the sensitive subject of the involvement of Sir Robert's brother in the housing development. Sir Robert is furious, brings the interview to an abrupt end, and threatens Sylvia.

Note   Planning permission for housing in England is a long and complicated business. It is very difficult to obtain in country areas. It increases the value of land enormously if there is planning permission. So, it would be scandalous for a minister to give such permission when he knows that the land belongs to a member of his family. It would almost certainly lead to his having to resign his government post.

The places mentioned in this story, such as Ledshire and Ledcombe, are imaginary.

The people in this episode

Sylvia is a radio reporter for a local news station, CRN. Here, she is doing a more important interview than she would normally because the senior journalist is ill. She is professional and decides to take a risk in this interview because she feels strongly about the issue. Jeff Coates would not be so persistent with Sir Robert or raise the subject of the MP's brother.

Sir Robert Firth is the local MP (Member of Parliament) and therefore has responsibilities for the constituents in the area, Ledshire East. His government post is Minister for the Environment. He starts by being rather patronizing but becomes extremely angry when he is skilfully driven into a corner by Sylvia.

● **Warm-up**   Look at the picture. Find out if the students know that it is a radio station. Ask:

What kind of programmes do your local radio stations broadcast?
Do your radio stations ever broadcast interviews with politicians?
What is Sylvia doing?
Does the person she is speaking to look comfortable with the situation?

Play the cassette. Ask: *Is it a friendly or a hostile interview?*

Play the cassette again, section by section.

Ask what happens and what the characters are doing or saying in each section. Look for key lines or questions that change the mood of the interview. Students should recognize the importance in the interview of questions like: *Have you spoken to local people yet? I understand that the farmland belongs to your brother?* Make sure the students notice when the interview begins to change in character.

Performance 1

COMPREHENSION

1 ○ ● **Explanation**   This is a true or false exercise, with questions on the whole text.

○ ● **Practice**   Students work in pairs to study the statements and write down their answers. See if they can answer any questions from memory before they look back at the text to find the answers.

A			
1 True	5 False	9 False	13 False
2 False	6 True	10 True	14 True
3 False	7 True	11 False	
4 True	8 False	12 True	

● **Extension**   To check students' answers, play the cassette again. Stop it after each section that contains the information for two or three of the statements. One student reads out a statement: *Jeff Coates works with Sylvia.* The class says *true* or *false.* Another student corrects a false statement and gives a reason: *The radio station is not near London because Sir Robert had to travel a long way from London for the interview.*

2 ○ ● **Explanation**   In the right order, these sentences make a summary of the interview.

● **Practice**   Look at each of the sentences with the students. Ask students what other information they can remember for each sentence.

Example

a *The critical report appeared in the local newspaper, the Ledshire Post.*

Students work in pairs to put each of the sentences into the correct order.

A										
1d	2g	3h	4a	5e	6i	7j	8b	9f	10c	11k

PRACTICE

1 ○ ● **Explanation**   This exercise practises irregular past participles and their pronunciation. It gives students an opportunity to practise finding this information in a dictionary.

○ ● **Practice**   Students may know some of these past participles and can use a dictionary to find the ones they do not know. If they do not have dictionaries with them, list the past participles on the board for them to match with the verbs in A and B. Students work individually to find the past participles. Then they can work in pairs to find as many rhyming pairs as possible. They may not know all of the pronunciations. If they have dictionaries they can look up the pronunciation of the words they do not know. They discuss their answers as a class.

A	**A**	
	see—seen	know—known
	buy—bought	send—sent
	catch—caught	feel—felt
	become—become	read—read
	give—given	sleep—slept
	speak—spoken	run—run
	sing—sung	teach—taught
	eat—eaten	make—made
	B win—won	be—been
	beat—beaten	kneel—knelt
	think—thought	ring—rung
	drive—driven	pay—paid
	fly—flown	bring—brought
	say—said	break—broken
	come—come	spend—spent
	keep—kept	fight—fought

Rhyming pairs
seen/been
bought/caught/taught/thought/brought/fought
become/come
spoken/broken
sent/spent
read/said
run/won
eaten/beaten
given/driven
known/flown
felt/knelt
slept/kept
sung/rung
made/paid

2a ○ ● **Explanation** This exercise gives practice in using the present perfect for 'news' events in the recent past, where the event itself is more important than *when* it happened.

○ ● **Practice** Students work individually to collect items of news about their jobs, studies, town or village, family and friends. Help students with the appropriate vocabulary:

find a job; change my job; get promotion
move to a new flat; build a new . . .
have a baby; find a new boyfriend/girlfriend; get married
buy a new . . .

Example
I've moved to a new house. My sister has passed her exams . . .

Students work in pairs to tell each other their news. In class, each student reports his or her partner's news: *. . . has moved to a new house. His/her sister has passed her exams. . . .*

b ○ ● **Explanation** Students practise writing a letter. They use the example to remind themselves how to lay it out correctly and how to begin and end it.

Note When you begin a letter with a title and a surname, e.g. *Dear Mr Brown*, you end the letter *Yours sincerely*. If the letter is to a good friend, you can end the letter *Yours* or *Love . . .*

● **Practice** Students use some of the news they practised in **a** to write a letter to a friend like the example in the book. They can do this exercise at home or in class.

3 ○ ● **Explanation** Students practise present perfect questions, though they may want to use other tenses, too.

○ ● **Practice** Students work in pairs to try to remember and write down Sylvia's questions in the interview, without looking at the text. They then study the text to check their ideas and find information for more questions she might have asked, as in the example.

○ ● **Extension** Students might like an opportunity to think up questions to ask a Minister for the Environment. In class, discuss current problems that affect your town or village and its environment. Then let students work in pairs or small groups to produce a list of questions. Students can compare their lists as a class. A radio interview role-play could be set up with one student as the interviewer and one as the politician. Pairs could perform their role-play in front of the class and the class then decides which politician gave the best answers.

4 ○ ● **Explanation** The two illustrations give the students the opportunity to use the present perfect to describe things that have (not) changed.

● **Practice** Students work in groups or pairs. They study the two pictures and note the differences. Then they write sentences like the examples to describe what has changed, and whether they think it's a good thing or a bad thing. Students read their sentences to the class. As a class, discuss whether the changes improve or spoil the village.

A **Sample answers**
They've changed the lights.
They've resurfaced the road.
They've built a supermarket.
They've cut down the trees.
They've changed the shop on the corner.

---

5 ○ ● **Explanation** Students listen to news headlines and a broadcast. They learn the new vocabulary associated with this news and then in **b** they have the opportunity to write their own news item. Introduce the new vocabulary before you play the cassette:

trade talks; delegates; reach an agreement; trade barriers; Minister of Education; different; technical subjects

Trade talks in Geneva have ended without agreement.

The Minister of Education has announced a new exam for 16-year-olds.

The trade talks between the Europeans and Americans in Geneva ended at lunch-time today. Delegates were not able to reach an agreement on trade barriers, but they have agreed to meet again next month.

There is going to be a new exam for 16-year-olds at school, the Minister of Education said today. All students have taken the same exams until now, but from next year they can take a different exam in technical subjects.

a ○ ● **Practice**   Students listen to the cassette, and then listen again, while following the printed text. Make sure everyone understands the two news items. Students work in small groups to pick out the verbs in the past simple and present perfect. They translate them and discuss why the tenses are used in each case. Discuss any problems as a class.

Note   In the first news item, the present perfect could have been used if there had been no mention of *when* the trade talks ended, i.e. *The trade talks between . . . have ended.* In the last sentence, the present perfect is used mainly for emphasis and the past simple is also correct: *but they agreed to meet again . . .*

b ○ ● Do this exercise orally before any writing begins. Encourage the students to use the present perfect.

PRONUNCIATION

1 ○ ● **Explanation**   As in Year 1, regular practice in word stress is vital for good communication. A spare moment at the end of a lesson is a good time to practise word stress and it's easy to make your own lists.

○ ● **Practice**   Students work in pairs to find the answers. Encourage them to use dictionaries to check their answers. Then let them practise saying the words.

A		
interview	**min**ister	go a**head**
government	**reg**ion	de**vel**opment
ac**cord**ing to	an**nounce**	**trans**port
taxpayer	ne**glec**ted	**crit**ical

2 ○ ● **Explanation**   Students practise the unstressed vowel sound /ə/. To make sure they recognize it, find a passage, e.g. the news items in exercise **5**, to do in class. Ask students to pick out the /ə/ sounds.

Note   *the* is pronounced /ðiː/ in front of a vowel.

○ ● **Practice**   Students work in pairs to find the answers. Check the answers as a class and give students a chance to say and hear the phrases correctly.

A
a lot of money   we'*re* providing th*e*m
f*o*r ye*a*rs   *a* list of questions
I've come fr*o*m Lond*o*n f*o*r the int*e*rview

READING

Explanation   This sequence of notes and memoranda shows what happens as a result of Sylvia's interview. Sam is both Jeff and Sylvia's boss. Sam seems to do what Jeff wants, and stops Sir Robert making trouble by dismissing Sylvia from her job. In fact, he supports Sylvia and finds her a better job, as a TV reporter.

Sir Robert resigns 'because of ill health'; the Prime Minister would allow a minister to resign rather than be dismissed because it looks better for the government.

● **Warm-up**   Students look quickly at the texts to answer the following questions:
How many people have written something?
Do we know all of them?
Does Jeff write to Sylvia?

○ ● **Practice**   The students read the texts to answer the comprehension questions. Check the answers as a class.

A	
1	Sir Robert wants apologies from Sylvia – one in writing, and one on the air.
2	No, he doesn't.
3	Sam is for Sylvia; Sir Robert and Jeff are against her.
4	Jeff doesn't get the apologies, but he gets what he wants because Sylvia loses her job with CRN.
5	Sir Robert has to resign from the government.

○ ● **Extension**   Students work in pairs or groups. They must imagine and write the memos that Sir Robert might have sent to Jeff and Sam, and to the Prime Minister about his resignation.

Options 1

GRAMMAR

Making generalizations

○ ● **Explanation**   A common way of making generalizations in English is to use *people* as the subject with a verb in the plural, e.g. *People need food and water to survive.* Read the examples together and make sure students understand the use of *people*. *People* can also be used with qualifying phrases:

People living in town . . .; people these days worry too much; and with quantifiers: *a few, some, many, a lot of, most.*

Note   It is not usual to say *all people*. Encourage students to use *everyone* instead.

a ● **Practice**   Students work alone. They use the pictures to make generalizations.

Examples
Most people like fruit.
A lot of people live in houses.
Some people prefer a flat to a house.
Many people don't like the beach.

b ● Students work in pairs or small groups to discuss their opinions. Then students compare their answers with the rest of the class. Alternatively, this can be done as a whole class activity, where students move around to interview as many people as possible.

NUMBERS

○ ● **Explanation**   Large numbers often present a problem. Students generally need practice in saying numbers quickly. The comma in the thousands is very important, for reasons of clarity. Speakers pause at this point.

Note   Students may already know that decimals in English use a point. 1,999, which is nearly two thousand, is very different from 1.999 (one point nine nine nine), which is nearly two.

● **Practice**   Students study the numbers, then work in pairs to practise saying and writing large numbers and prices.

GRAMMAR AND VOCABULARY

○ ● **Explanation**   This exercise will extend students' vocabulary. They can test themselves against the clock to see how many words they can think of, e.g. in two minutes. To make it more difficult, they could think of countable and uncountable nouns.

○ ● **Practice**   Students work in groups with one person writing the words down. After the time limit, the groups can compare answers to see which has the most words.

A   **Possible answers**

Furniture	C	tables, chairs, sofas, wardrobes
	U	wood, metal, cloth
Money	C	coins, notes, dollars, cheques, credit cards
	U	wealth, credit
Food	C	eggs, rolls, saucepans, plates, forks, apples
	U	bread, cheese, meat, fish, wine
News	C	journalists, newspapers, programmes, headlines, stories
	U	information, drama

SMALL TALK

○ ● **Explanation**   This kind of exchange is very useful for students when they have visitors from abroad, or when they are travelling abroad themselves. Food is always a good topic of conversation, and students should be able to talk readily about the food specialities of their country/area.

First ask the students to talk about food from their area: *What dishes do you recommend to a visitor in a typical restaurant in your country?*

Ask students to describe a typical dish in detail: *What are the main ingredients? How do you prepare and cook the dish?*

In class, build up some useful cooking terms, e.g. *fry, grill, roast, boil.*

● **Practice**   In pairs, students continue the dialogue that is started in their books. They can present their dialogue to the class.

TIME

a ○ ● **Explanation**   Students practise time phrases and note-writing. There is a lot of practice with the use of the present continuous tense with a future time phrase to describe future planned activities.

● **Practice**   Students work in pairs. They know that 'today' is the 25th. They work backwards and forwards from the 25th to complete the diary, with the key words from the sentences given.

A		
22 Sunday		*Cinema with Bob*
23 Monday		
24 Tuesday		*Visit Aunt Josie*
25 Wednesday		*English exam*
26 Thursday		*Lunch with Herbert*
27 Friday		
28 Saturday		*Dinner with Grace*
29 Sunday		
30 Monday		
1 Tuesday		*Tennis with Grace*
		Mum's birthday
2 Wednesday		
3 Thursday		*Lunch with Susan*
		Holidays start
4 Friday		*Dentist*
		Leaving for Spain

● **Extension**   Students ask and answer questions about the completed information in the diary.

Example

A *When is Jill going on holiday?*
B *She's going on holiday on the 4th of May.*

B *What is she doing on Tuesday, the first of May?*
A *She's playing tennis with Grace.*

To make things more difficult, the student who answers must not look at the information, but try and remember.

b ● Students describe what they are doing at the weekend in note form in their diary. Some ideas are given to help them.

c ● Students practise asking and answering about what they are doing next week.

2
Preview

1 *will/won't*

○ ● **Explanation**   This unit teaches the use of *will* and *won't*. The main uses are introduced here:
to talk about the future
to make a promise
to make a prediction
to make a spontaneous decision

These uses can be discussed at the end of exercise **1**.

a ○ ● **Warm-up**   Read the text as a class and give the students an opportunity to try to translate the first two sentences. Check that the students recognize which tense it is. Write the full and short forms of *will* on the board, or get a volunteer from the class:
*will   'll
will not   won't*

○ ● **Practice**   Students read the text alone or in pairs to make sure they understand it. They write the translation of the first two sentences and compare their answers with the rest of the class.

b   Students work in their pairs to find examples for the different forms of *will* and *won't*.

A	Sample answers	
	A first person	*I'll have a cup of tea ready.*
	A second person	*You will see the entrance to Longthorpe.*
	A third person	*He'll tell you where I am.*
	A negative	*You won't see the castle at first.*
	A question	*Will you be ready soon?*

Still in pairs, students discuss the three questions at the end of **b** before checking the answers as a class.

A	1 The text is part of a letter.
	2 Its purpose is to give Max and Poppy directions to get to Archie's castle.
	3 Archie wrote the letter. Max is reading it to Poppy, who asks him to give it to her to look after.

○ ● **Practice**   Students can now look at the different uses of *will* and *won't*. Read the explanation in column 2. Make sure the students understand the four uses described here. Do the exercise at the bottom of the column as a class so you can discuss the answers.

A	1c 2a 3b

2 *going to* (inevitability)

○ ● **Explanation**   In Year 1 we studied the use of *going to* to express a planned future event: *I'm going to play squash this evening.* We also use *going to* to make a prediction for which we have present evidence, i.e. it looks inevitable that something will happen. Here students learn to use *going to* to make predictions. They look at the pictures and work out or predict what is going to happen.

● **Practice**   Look at the first picture and ask: *What is going to happen?* Students answer: *He's going to sneeze.* Students work in pairs to predict what is going to happen in each picture. They then check their answers in class.

A

2 The glass is going to fall.
3 The woman is going to win.
4 It's going to rain.
5 She's going to catch the ball.
6 He's going to open his present.

● **Extension** To give students further practice, mime some actions and ask: *What am I going to do?* Students can then answer: *You're going to . . . .* Examples: *You're going to laugh, cry, read, pay, phone somebody,* etc. Make sure that the actions show that you are *about* to do something, i.e. do not show the completed actions.

3 Comparative adjectives

a ○ ● **Explanation** Students learn regular comparative adjectives.

● **Warm-up** Read the list of adjectives and make sure students can pronounce the words correctly. Read out one positive adjective at a time (i.e. not the comparative forms) and ask a student to point to a noun that fits the description. As a class, do one matching example with both the positive and comparative forms: *a small cat; a smaller cat.*

○ ● **Practice** Students work out the rest of the exercise in pairs. They match the adjectives with the correct pictures and compare their answers in class.

A

1 a small cat	2 a big dog
a smaller cat	a bigger dog
3 a tall man	4 a comfortable chair
a taller man	a more comfortable chair
a thin man	a wide chair
a thinner man	a wider chair

b ○ ● **Explanation** Students learn the rules for comparative forms.

○ ● **Presentation** Look at the groups of adjectives and their comparatives. Ask students what they notice about the comparative forms first in **a**, then in **b**, **c**, and **d**. Let students discuss a rule for each. Do the same for groups 2 and 3. These are the three regular groups. There are a number of irregular comparatives which students will have to learn. Only two are given here.

○ ● **Practice** Students work in pairs to write a rule for each, if possible, giving other examples for each group.

A See the Grammar Summary on page 27.

c ○ ● **Explanation** Students practise the form of the comparative adjective + *than* to compare things.

○ ● **Practice** The students look at the pictures in **a** and make full sentences about them.

● **Extension** For further practice you can let the students compare themselves with their neighbour in a chain around the class: *I am taller/older/ shorter/younger than . . .* Give the first example comparing yourself with the first student; that student reports what you have said, then makes a comparison between himself/herself and his/her neighbour, and so on round the class.

Example

A *I am taller than B.*
B *A is taller than me.*
  I am older than C.
C *B is older than me.*
  I am . . .

4 Direction expressions

a ○ ● **Explanation** Students learn expressions for giving directions. In this matching exercise, they find the symbol that fits the English expression and then they give the translation in their language.

○ ● **Practice** Students work in pairs to do **a** and then compare their answers with the class.

A 1g 2f 3j 4h 5b 6e 7a 8d 9c 10i

b ○ ● **Explanation** Students use the expressions they learnt in **a** to practise giving directions.

● **Practice** Look at the map together. Find the list of places on the map with the students. Read the example and do another example if you feel the students need extra help. Then let students work in pairs. They should take turns in asking for and giving directions from the post office to the different places. Each pair can have a turn asking for and giving directions in front of the class.

In the dark

In this scene Poppy and Max are on their way by car to Longthorpe Castle to visit Archie. They are using a small secondary road because Poppy doesn't like the motorway. They take a wrong turn and end up on a farm track. The car breaks down, so they walk to a nearby village. On the way, Max sprains his ankle. They get to a hotel, where they stay for the night. The next day Max tries to get his son Hank to fetch them. He can't do it as he's working for his exams, so Poppy rings Toby, who offers to come. She gives him detailed directions to the hotel.

The people in this episode

Poppy is definitely in charge. She makes the decision about their route and blames Max when they get lost. She is scornful of Max when he wants to check under the bonnet of the car and tells him bluntly not to bother since he doesn't know anything about cars. She fixes up the room for them, and is exasperated with Max for not remembering Hank's exams. She arranges for Toby to come instead – she isn't bothered by the fact that she used to be Toby's girlfriend.

Max is not as forceful as he used to be – at least where Poppy is concerned. In this scene he allows himself to be talked out of going on the motorway, and ends up with a sprained ankle. He disapproves of Poppy ringing Toby, but she takes no notice.

The hotelier is courteous and helpful.

● **Warm up**   Look at the picture. Ask:

What's happening?
Where are they?
Why are they there?

Play the cassette of the whole episode first. Then play the cassette section by section. For each section ask:

Where are Poppy and Max?
What's happening?
or *What has happened?*
How is Poppy/Max behaving?

Performance 2

COMPREHENSION

1 ○ ● **Explanation**   Students test their comprehension of the story. The true or false exercise refers to the whole episode.

○ ● **Practice**   Study the statements as a class. Then play the cassette and stop it after each section that contains the information for two or three of the statements. One student reads out a statement and the class comes to an agreement about whether it is true or false. If the statement is false, another student corrects it.

A	1 True
	2 False (Poppy finds the route on the road atlas.)
	3 True
	4 True
	5 False (They are one mile from Merlock, a village.)
	6 True
	7 False (They walk to a hotel.)
	8 False (Max has sprained his ankle.)
	9 True
	10 False (Max rings Hank, Poppy rings Toby.)
	11 True

2 ○ ● **Explanation**   In this vocabulary exercise, the students try to work out meaning from context. Encourage them to do a final check with a dictionary if they need to.

○ ● **Practice**   Students work in pairs to find the phrase in the text and discuss the meaning. They then translate the phrases. Discuss the answers in class.

3 ○ ● **Explanation**   Students have the chance to give their opinions on the characters. This is an oral fluency exercise.

● **Practice**   Help students by writing the names on the board and asking students to suggest adjectives they associate with each character. Students should explain their suggestion, or give a sentence from the text which illustrates it. Alternatively, students discuss in pairs or small groups and a spokesperson for each group tells the class their conclusions. The class compares views.

Possible answers

Max is weak, indecisive (*What'll we do now?*), and thoughtless. (He makes a decision to phone his son who is preparing for exams.)
Poppy is bossy, decisive, domineering, critical, and inconsiderate. (She does what she wants without considering other people's feelings, needs, or preferences.) In their relationship Poppy has become the domineering wife and Max the 'hen-pecked' husband.

PRACTICE

1 ○ ● **Explanation** In this exercise, students identify *will/won't* sentences according to the three types in Preview 1.

○ ● **Practice** Let students work in pairs to find examples of *will/won't* sentences in the story. Then, as a class, decide whether they fit into any of these categories: a prediction, a promise, or a spontaneous decision.

Note Not all of the *will/won't* sentences fit into these three categories. There are also examples of talking about the future, questions, and negatives as in the Preview. There is also an example of offering to do something: *I'll give you a hand with those bags*, and a request: *Will you go to Lion Place?* (See the Grammar Summary on page 27.)

A

Future	A prediction
What'll we do now?	It'll be much prettier . . .
The car won't be ready today.	The car won't start. That won't help.
A promise	**A decision**
I'll ask Dave to have a look at it.	We'll go on the motorway. I'll look at the road atlas.

2 a○ ● **Explanation** Students imagine themselves in Poppy and Max's situation to practise *will* for expressing decisions.

○ ● **Practice** Look at the pictures together and discuss what they mean and what the choices are. Students work in small groups to write a sentence for each picture. They must use *will* or *won't* to express the decision and they should add a context for each, like the example.

A **Possible answers**

1 We'll have lunch at the first restaurant we see.
2 We won't go to the information office because we have instructions from Archie.
3 We'll stop for petrol in a town about half way.
4 We'll stop for coffee in an attractive village.
5 We won't take food for a picnic along the way.
6 We'll find a gift shop in one of the towns and buy a present for Archie.
7 We won't go to the Museum of Farming on this trip.
8 We'll visit the 14th century abbey on the way.

● **Extension** Students report their answers to the class using the third person plural.

Example

They'll have lunch at the first restaurant they see.
They won't go to the information office, etc.

b○ ● **Explanation** This is a free exercise. Students use the symbols in **a** to make up short conversations between Max and Poppy as in the example. Students should consider the personalities of Max and Poppy in each conversation, e.g: They could have Poppy being aggressive and Max being defensive, or Poppy being tired and Max being cross; Poppy thinking about money and spending, and Max wanting to spend money on Poppy.

● **Practice** Students should work in groups to make the conversations. They could then work in pairs to prepare one conversation each to act for the class.

3 a○ ● **Explanation** This is a gap-filling exercise that gives practice with prepositions.

○ ● **Practice** Students do the exercise in pairs first, then check the answers orally in class.

A You leave the A54 *at* Maud's Silford and go on *to* the B5112. The road passes *through* some lovely scenery after this. *On* the left, the river runs *close to* the road *for* several miles, then you come *to* a bridge. Go straight *over* the bridge, and take the first turning *on* the right. Go *past* the old sawmill, *past* the Crown Hotel and *through* the village of Long March. *After* three miles, you come *to* the town *of* Naseby St Paul.

b○ ● **Explanation** Here is further practice of the language used to give directions.

● **Practice** Students work in groups to prepare the directions to King's Silford. They have to work backwards but all the language they need is in exercise **a**. Let students from each group give the directions to the class while the class follows on the map to check them. Students can write out the directions for homework using **3a** as an example.

A **Possible answer**
You leave Naseby St Paul and after three miles you come to the village of Long March. Go through the village, past the Crown Hotel and the old sawmill, and take the first turning on the left. Go over the bridge and the road passes through some lovely scenery after this. On the right, the river runs close to the road for several miles. Then leave the B5112 and turn left on to the A54 at Maud's Silford. After a mile or so, you come to King's Silford.

4a○ ● **Explanation** This is an exercise to practise making comparisons.

● **Practice** Study the pictures with the students and use the adjectives to describe the bungalows and the cottage separately.

Examples

The cottage has an untidy garden.
The bungalow is modern but not attractive.

Then make up some examples that compare them:

The cottage garden is untidier than the bungalow garden.

Then let the students work in groups to see how many comparisons they can make in three minutes. Compare answers as a class.

b ● **Practice** Students work individually at first to write a short description about one or two buildings they are familiar with. Help them with vocabulary. Then students work in pairs. They use the information to compare the buildings. If students are from the same place, make sure they choose different buildings. Alternatively, the students can compare two different towns or cities.

5○ ● **Explanation** Here students learn to make enquiries about the future using *will*.

○ ● **Practice** Discuss ideas with students about clothes, the weather, what hotels provide and don't provide. Give a few examples before using the expressions given:

Will I need warm clothes?
Will it be very cold?

Let students work in small groups to prepare their questions. As a class, they then compare their lists.

● **Extension** Students use their list of questions to do a role-play. One student is the worried customer, the other the reassuring travel agent. Let them improvise, if they can, without looking at their notes.

6○ ● **Explanation** Students practise postcard writing, and making comparisons.

○ ● **Practice** Look at the postcard. Draw the students' attention to the layout and compare it to the layout of a letter. Discuss with the students what they could say about living in a Scottish castle which would interest their friends. Possible topics are: the weather, people, countryside, food, clothes. They compare these with their country. Students can write their postcards at home or in class.

7○ ● **Explanation** Students need to work out what Toby's questions are since they only hear Poppy's replies.

○ ● **Practice** Students work in pairs to complete the dialogue.

● **Extension** Put some prompts for the dialogue on the board, e.g. *Greeting; Where?; Reason for telephone call; Max?; Help?; Where exactly?; Saying goodbye.* Students in pairs can try to recreate the conversation from memory, using the prompts list.

A **Possible answer**
Toby Hello?
Poppy Toby? Hi, Poppy here.
Toby Poppy? Where are you?
Poppy We're at a place called Merlock.
Toby Why are you there?/What are you doing there?
Poppy We broke down last night, and Max has sprained his ankle.

Toby	How is he?
Poppy	He's fine, thank you.
Toby	Do you want me to come and get you?
Poppy	You *are* kind.
Toby	Where is Merlock?
Poppy	It's off the A912. You go across the roundabout, and through the village. Then you go past a pub, and the hotel is up the steep hill on the left.
Toby	Which hotel is it?/What is the hotel called?
Poppy	It's the Merlock Manor Hotel.
Toby	I'll leave now. Bye.
Poppy	Bye, darling.

PRONUNCIATION

1 ○ ● **Explanation** As with word stress, using correct sentence stress is vital for effective communication in English. Using the wrong sentence stress can give a sentence an entirely different meaning.

● **Practice** Play the cassette and let students listen and identify the sentences. Play the cassette again for students to underline the main stress. Play the cassette a third time for students to check their answers.

T.2.2
A

1 I don't **like** the motorway.
2 Country roads are more **interesting** than motorways.
3 This road is a **scenic** route.
4 Where **are** we?
5 **I've** left it at home!
6 How **far** is it from here?
7 The **car** won't start.

2 ○ ● **Explanation** English vowel sounds have numerous different spellings. This exercise revises some of the more difficult ones.

● **Practice** Read the words to the students once. Then let them work in pairs to identify the words that have the same vowel sound as the first word in each group. They can use a dictionary to check their answers before they discuss them as a class.

A

1 *short* route *caught walked thought* road *bought*
2 *more* through *door* who are *four tour* (also /tʊə(r)/) you are
3 *can't* want *aren't* don't *plant danced*

LISTENING

Travel news

1 ○ ● **Explanation** This listening task requires students to listen for information.

 ○ ● **Warm-up** Students first look at the map and pick out the place names.

● **Practice** Play the cassette and ask students to listen only for the place names. They must underline or write down only the places on the map which are mentioned on the recording.

A

(Derbyshire), Brailsford, Foston, Ashbourne, Leek, Great Cubley.

2 ○ ● Look at the road signs as a class and discuss their meanings (see answers). Play the cassette again. This time, the students number the road signs.

A

3 (blocked road)	6 (diversion)	2 (heavy snow)
4 (roadworks)	7 (heavy load)	5 (single line traffic)
	8 (heavy traffic)	1 (fog)

T.2.3

And now, travel news in your area.
There is thick fog throughout the region, and the police ask motorists to take great care. Heavy snow will reach Derbyshire this afternoon, and this will make conditions very difficult.
An accident has blocked the A52 at Brailsford.
There are road-works at Foston on the A50. Single lane traffic is in operation.
In Ashbourne, there are diversions in the town centre as the A515 to the north is closed for drainage works.
There will be a slow-moving heavy load travelling from Ashbourne to Leek between ten and twelve this morning.
There is heavy traffic at Great Cubley because of a School Open Day.

READING

- ○ ● **Explanation** This is a text from a tourist guide to a village in Derbyshire. If possible, show where Derbyshire is on a map of England. Note the pronunciation /dɑːbɪʃə/.

- ○ ● **Warm-up** Pre-teach vocabulary:

  stone and brick   divide   according to
  rules   apart   free-for-all
  main street   scorer

  Ask students to read through the text. Ask:

  What kind of text is it?
  Who is it for?
  Where would you read it?
  Why is this information in this text?

1 ○ ● **Practice** Students look at the pictures and match them to the word or phrase.

A	1b	2b	3c	4b	5a	6b

2 ○ ● Students answer the true/false questions on the text. If this exercise is done in class, ask why the 'false' answers are wrong.

A	
	1 False (Ashbourne is right next to the Peak District National Park.)
	2 False (A tributary of the River Dove, Henmore Brook, runs through Ashbourne.)
	3 True
	4 False (The football match starts on a Tuesday.)
	5 False (Each team comes from one side of Henmore Brook.)
	6 False (There aren't many rules but there are some.)
	7 True
	8 True

- ● **Extension** To check students' understanding of the text, ask them to retell it in their own words to the rest of the class, who can interrupt and correct.

3   **Measurements**

- ○ ● **Explanation** The old measurements, i.e. the imperial measurements, are still widely used in Britain and in North America, so it may be useful for students to be familiar with them.

Imperial measurements
12 inches = 1 foot
3 feet = 1 yard
1760 yards = 1 mile

- ○ ● **Practice** Put the students in groups to see how many questions they can answer before explaining them to the class.

A	
	1 Longer
	2 Yes (e.g. the USA)
	3 Smaller (It is 0.0833 feet.)
	4 Bigger (It is 3 feet.)
	5 A metre. A metre is longer than a yard; it equals about 1 yard and 3 inches.
	6 Divide by 5 and multiply by 8.

Options 2

VOCABULARY

- ○ ● **Explanation** This exercise is to practise vocabulary from the unit.

- ● **Practice** Students write down all the words they can associate with travelling by car.

- ● **Extension** You can do this exercise as word associations in a chain round the class. One student says the first word they can think of, the next student says the first word they can think of associated with that word, and so on round the class. Alternatively, write key words in the middle of the board, e.g. *weather, roads, food*, and let the students write words with pleasant associations above, e.g. *sunshine, smooth/empty, five-star restaurant*, and negative words below, e.g. *storm, traffic jam, closed*. Students can then write a short dialogue between Poppy and Max with as many of the words as possible included.

TRANSLATION

- ○ ● **Explanation** These hotel notices would be found in all English-speaking countries and also in many international hotels.

- ○ ● **Practice** Students think about the way such notices are phrased in their own language and suggest other signs hotels use.

GRAMMAR

○ ● **Explanation** This exercise practises the use of *will* and *shall* to make offers.

● **Practice** Read the examples and make sure the students understand this use of *will/shall*. Students work alone or in pairs to make offers for each statement.

A **Sample answers**
1 I'll make you a coffee.
2 Shall I make you a drink?
3 I'll carry one of them for you.
4 Shall I try?
5 Shall I help you?
6 I'll lend you some.
7 Shall I do it for you?
8 I'll get you an indigestion tablet.

Then students work in groups to think up mini-dramas, as in the example. They think of two or three situations and create the dialogue for each one.

TRAVELLING 1

a ○ ● **Explanation** Students practise the language needed to ask for a hotel room.

● **Practice** Students listen to the cassette and fill in the gaps. Play the cassette again for students to check their answers.

T.2.4

A
1 A Good afternoon.
　B Good afternoon. Have you got a *single room*?
　A How *long for*?
　B *Three nights*.
　A With *a bath* or *shower*?
　B A *shower*, please.
2 A We'd like *a double room* with *a shower* for *three nights, please*.
　B Room 37, sir. Here's your *key*.
3 A Good morning. *We'd like* a room, please.
　B A *double* room?
　A Yes, please.
　B *I've got* a room with twin beds. Is that all right?
　A Yes. *Has it got* a shower?
　B No, it's *got* a bath.
　A That's OK.
　B *How long* are you staying?
　A Two nights. Till Tuesday.

b ● Students summarize what each traveller asks for. They compare their answers in class.

A
1 They want a single room with a shower for three nights.
2 They want a double room with a shower for three nights.
3 They want a double room with a shower for two nights, and they get a room with twin beds and a bath for two nights.

c ○ ● Students improvise their own dialogues like the ones in **a**, using the information provided. They should take it in turns to be the traveller and the receptionist. Allow pairs to act out at least one dialogue for the class, if they want.

TRAVELLING 2

Guidebooks

○ ● **Explanation** Students write an entry in a guide book for an imaginary place called Merlock.

○ ● **Practice** Read the entry for Lydford and discuss what kind of place Merlock sounds like. Then using the text in their book as an example, students write their own descriptions. They compare answers with other students.

A **Possible answer**
Merlock. Village off the A912, nice scenery, hilly farming area. One pub, post office.
Interesting sights: Old church, pretty cottages.
Accommodation: Merlock Manor Hotel: 15 rooms, 5 double, 10 single (all with shower or bath). Tel: 0876 1640. Car park for 12 cars.
Access: go through the village on the A912, and the hotel is on the road on the left up the hill.
Proprietors: Mr and Mrs Fenwick.

FURTHER PRACTICE

○ ● **Explanation** This is a scanning for information reading exercise.

○ ● **Practice** Students calculate the answers from the information on the bill. They can work alone or in pairs and check their answers with the rest of the class.

A
1 Two	5 Wine
2 For three nights	6 No
3 £53 a night	7 Garage
4 Yes	

3
Preview

1 Vocabulary

a ○ ● **Explanation**   Students will know some of the vocabulary that describes parts of a house or building but they probably won't know all of it. This exercise introduces new house vocabulary and the grammar *to need to do something*.

○ ● **Warm-up**   Look at the picture of the house and check the pronunciation of the new words. Make sure they understand collective terms, e.g. *woodwork, wiring, plumbing,* etc.

● **Practice**   Students work in pairs. They discuss each part of the house and fill in their chart to say whether it is in good or bad condition. Students check their answers with the rest of the class.

A | House checklist

Outside	Good	Bad
walls		√
roof		√
gutters	√	
drains		√
chimney	√	
Inside		
woodwork		√
floor		√
windows	√	
plumbing		√
central heating	√	
wiring		√

b ○ ● **Explanation**   This exercise practises the use of the verb *to need to do something* where *need* has the same meaning as 'it is necessary' but without the sense of obligation of *to have to do something* which students learn in exercise **2**.

○ ● **Presentation**   All the parts of the house that are in bad condition will need attention. They will need to be replaced, repaired, or painted. Those parts that are in good condition won't need to be checked. Some parts may need to be replaced because they are inadequate, or old-fashioned.

○ ● **Warm-up**   Read the list of words and make sure students understand the difference in meaning. They should use a dictionary to ensure they understand the words. Then discuss the checklist and ask students what the owner needs to do about each part. Students use the example to help them.

● **Practice**   Students work in pairs to produce a list of what the owner *needs* or *doesn't need to do*. They compare their lists as a class.

A | **Possible answers**
He/She needs to repair and paint the walls.
He/She needs to repair the roof.
He/She doesn't need to check the gutters.
He/She needs to check and repair the drains.
He/She needs to repair the woodwork.
He/She needs to repair the floors.
He/She doesn't need to replace the windows.
He/She needs to check and replace the plumbing.
He/She doesn't need to check the central heating.
He/She needs to check and replace the wiring.

2 *have/has to, don't/doesn't have to*

○ ● **Explanation**   *Have to* expresses obligation. This exercise helps students practise the positive and negative use of *have to* where there is necessity as in *need to*, but without choice.

a ● **Warm-up**   Ask students to think about all the things they (don't) have to do today. Read the examples together to give them ideas.

- **Practice**   Students work in pairs using *have to* and *don't have to*. Each student tells her/his partner one thing that they have to do and one thing they don't have to do for each day of the week.

Example

On Monday I have to practise for my piano lesson. I don't have to get up early because college starts late.

The partner has to write down what her/his partner says and report to the class:

On Monday, Patricia has to practise the piano. She doesn't have to get up early because college starts late.

b ○ ● **Warm-up**   Look at the pictures and identify each of the people: *a secretary, a doctor, a student, a shop assistant, a survey interviewer, a waiter*. Read the verbs together and ask students to match them with the likely person.

- **Practice**   Students make sentences describing what each person has to do, as in the example. Then they say one thing that each person does not have to do.

A **Possible answers**

A secretary has to type letters. A secretary doesn't have to examine patients.
A doctor has to examine patients. A doctor doesn't have to sell things.
A student has to study. A student doesn't have to serve customers.
A shop assistant has to serve customers. A shop assistant doesn't have to travel.
A survey interviewer has to travel. A survey interviewer doesn't have to serve customers.
A waiter has to serve customers. A waiter doesn't have to type.

3   *should/shouldn't*

○ ● **Explanation**   Students are introduced to the use of *should* to ask for or give advice, or to express an opinion or make a suggestion.

○ ● **Warm-up**   Look at the pictures and discuss what is happening.

- **Practice**   Ask students to give each person in the picture advice like the example.

A **Possible answers**
2 You should have a rest.
3 You should buy an umbrella.
4 You should take your washing to a laundrette.

- **Extension**   Students work in pairs to think of other advice they might offer the people in the pictures. They share their ideas with the class.

A **Possible answers**
1 She should go and lie down.
2 He should have a holiday.
3 She should go into a café until the rain has stopped.
4 He should buy a washing machine.

Students can also mime a problem to a group which then decides what the problem is and gives him/her advice. Or students can write down problems on pieces of paper which are then collected in and redistributed to pairs or groups so that they can write their advice underneath.

4   Present perfect with *for* and *since*

○ ● **Presentation**   When we want to describe a period of time that started in the past and continues up to the present, we use the present perfect tense (*I have worked here . . .*) and *for* or *since*. *For* tells us *how long*, e.g. a few days, two years, etc., *since* tells us the point in the past when the period began, e.g. January, 1967, last week.

- **Practice**   Read the two sentences. Ask:

*Which sentence shows a period of time? (**for** six months)*
*Which sentence shows a point in time? (**since** January)*

Ask questions to practise *for* and *since*, for example:

How long have you lived in . . .?
How long have you studied English?
How long have you worked at your present job? etc.

Students give their answers using *for* for periods of time, e.g. I've studied English **for** *two years;* or *since* if they want to describe when the activity began, e.g. *I've worked in my present job **since** March last year.*

b ○ ● Students work in pairs to find the answers and check them with the rest of the class.

A	for four months	since 15th July
	since March	since Tuesday
	for two years	since 1981
	for ten days	for three weeks

5 Present perfect with *ever/never* versus past simple

○ ● **Presentation** We use *ever* with the present perfect when we are asking about something that has happened during someone's life up until now, e.g.

Have you ever been to Tibet?
Have you ever tasted dried meat?

Never says that something hasn't happened in your life, up until now:

No, I've never been to Tibet.
No, I've never tasted dried meat.

We use the past simple to refer to a particular time, e.g. *Did you go to the cinema last night? No, I didn't.*

We use the present perfect to ask and answer about something without a particular time reference, e.g. *Have you seen the new Madonna film? Yes, I have.* But if we want to answer *when*, we use the past simple: *Yes, I saw it last night.*

○ ● **Warm-up** Read the examples as a class and make sure students understand the role of the present perfect tense and the meaning of *ever/never*. Look at the first picture and ask for a dialogue like the examples.

● **Practice** When you are sure that the students understand the use of *Have you ever . . .?*, and the differences between it and the past simple, let students work in pairs to produce a dialogue for each picture. They can read out one of their dialogues for the class.

A **Possible answers**

A Have you ever seen a flying saucer?/a purple cow?/a vampire?/a ghost? (1, 5, 6, 7)
B No, I've never seen one.
A Have you ever ridden in a hot-air balloon?/on a double-decker bus? (4, 8)
B No, I haven't./Yes, I rode on one last year when I was in London.
A Have you ever climbed up the Eiffel Tower? (2)
B No, but I have seen it.
A Have you ever seen/read *Gone with the Wind*? (3)
B No, I haven't./Yes, I have.

6 Money

a ○ ● **Explanation** This is a vocabulary and dictionary exercise about money.

○ ● **Warm-up** Read the list of words and make sure students can pronounce them.

○ ● **Practice** Students work in pairs or small groups to sort the words into the appropriate columns. They check their answers with the rest of the class. Some of the words can go in more than one column. Let the students give examples to explain their decisions.

A **Possible answer**

Banking	Cash	Business	
bank manager	fiver	sell	get rich
interest	tenner	debt	borrow
ten per cent		buy	make money
(borrow)		pay back	owe
(owe)		tax	
(pay back)		businessman/woman	

b ○ ● **Explanation** In order to do this exercise, students must understand the words in italics, which are also concerned with money.

○ ● **Warm-up** Read the sentences in column **A** and make sure students understand them. Encourage students to use a dictionary wherever necessary. These words appear in the soap so they will see them again in context.

○ ● **Practice** Students work in pairs to match up the sentences in **A** with the right one from **B**. They check their answers as a class.

A

When you support your children, you look after them and pay for everything they need.

When his father died, Archie inherited the castle, so it belongs to him now.

My aunt died last year. In her will she left me £500.

Be careful! That table is very valuable. It's 400 years old. If you break it, you will have to pay.

Tax is money you have to pay the government on salaries and property.

Waiter! Please bring me the bill. I finished my meal half an hour ago. I'm waiting to pay.

If a shop charges too much, everything in it is very expensive.

Death duties are tax that rich people's families have to pay the government when they die.

An Englishman's home (is his castle)

T.3.1 Tom arrives unexpectedly at Longthorpe Castle on his motorbike. Archie tells him he will probably have to sell the castle. Tom is horrified, especially when he learns that it's been in Archie's family for about seven hundred years. He advises him to open the house to the public, sell some land, or borrow money from the bank. These aren't practical solutions for Archie. Archie tells Tom about the lost Longthorpe treasure. (During the Civil War in the 17th century, a lot of the King's supporters sold their goods to raise money. The King – Charles I – lost the war, and was beheaded in 1649.) But in any case, he says he's going to need more than some gold and silver plates to do all the necessary repairs. Tom has a look at the boiler for Archie, because the heating isn't very efficient. While they are having a snack, and looking at the priest's hole, the boiler blows up. Part of the wall is blown away, and they find the Longthorpe treasure hidden there.

The people in this episode

Archie has to pay death duties – these would be relative to the value of the castle and lands, and he would have to sell the property in order to get the money to pay the tax. He is alone, many of the rooms are shut up, and the heating doesn't work very well. With all this, it isn't surprising that he's feeling a bit depressed.

Tom is energetic and full of suggestions. He is surprised to find that an aristocrat who owns a castle is so hard up and owns nothing valuable. He tries to be helpful by fixing the boiler. He obviously gets on with Archie, and is, as always, very straightforward in saying what he thinks and feels.

● **Warm-up**   Look at the picture. Ask:

Who are the people?
Where do you think they are?
What has happened?
What are they looking at?
Why are they in that room?
Do they look frightened? Happy? Surprised?

Play the cassette. Ask the students:

What two main things happen?
Does one event lead to another?

Play the cassette again, section by section. Ask the students what has happened in each section.

Suggested check questions:

Has Archie's family lived in the castle for a long time?
What was the Longthorpe treasure? What happened to it?
Who should Archie talk to?
What is the boiler room? Why is Tom surprised by it?
Where are they? What are they looking at?
What's happened, and what have they found?

Performance 3

COMPREHENSION

1 ○ ● **Explanation**   This is a gap-filling exercise that summarizes the whole text.

   ○ ● **Practice**   Do the exercise orally first, as a retelling exercise. You can begin by asking students to suggest key words, e.g. *treasure, bad condition*, and writing these on the board as cues. You can add some more prompts, e.g. *sell, borrow*. Then get the students to retell the story round the class, each student adding a sentence until complete. Then they can gap fill the exercise.

A   Tom arrives at Longthorpe Castle. He has come *by bike*. Archie is worried. The castle is in bad *condition* and he thinks he'll have to *sell* it. Tom says he *shouldn't* sell it. He should sell some *land* for housing, or *open* the house to the *public*. Archie tells Tom about the Longthorpe *treasure*. He says it *disappeared* in the 17th century. Tom tells him he should talk to his *bank manager* and *borrow* money from the bank for repairs. But Archie doesn't know how he can make *money* to pay it back. Tom says he's *hungry* and cold, so Archie goes to the *kitchen* to prepare some food. Tom says he*'ll have* a look at the central *heating*. It's very old and doesn't work. Tom is a *plumber*. After the meal, Archie *shows* Tom the house. They are looking at the *priest's hole* in the *dining* room when there is a loud noise. The *boiler* has exploded. They go to the boiler room – and find the Longthorpe *treasure*. It's in a *hole* in the *wall*.

2 ○ ● **Explanation**   These are vocabulary exercises. Students should use the context to help work out the meaning of any unfamiliar expressions.

a ○ ● **Practice**   These are common colloquial expressions. Students work in small groups. First they find the words in the text and then they work out the answers.

A   *some place:* a grand or impressive place. Both words are emphatic. *Some* can be used with other nouns in a similar way, e.g. *That was some meal:* That was a wonderful meal.
   a fiver: A five-pound note (They should remember this from the vocabulary exercise in the Preview.)

cheer up: don't be sad; stop being sad.
grub: food (The word has been slang for 300 years.)

b ○ ● Many of these words are in the text. Students should use the text and a dictionary to distinguish between the pairs of words. They can work in pairs or small groups.

A   *house:* the building; *housing:* a group of houses for people to live in; houses in general.
   clear things up: to sort out problems and settle any difficulties;
   tidy things up: to put things away and put things in order.
   land: in this context, the area of ground owned by a person especially around their house;
   country: the opposite of town areas, where the land is mostly for farming, forests, etc.
   heirloom: any object that a family has possessed for more than one generation. It doesn't have to be valuable;
   treasure: a collection of valuable, precious things.
   goblet: a glass or metal drinking container with a stem and no handle;
   glass: a normal drinking utensil made of glass, with or without stem, and without a handle.
   civil war: a war between groups of people inside the same country;
   world war: a war between many different countries.
   ancient: centuries old; *old:* not new.
   plaster: the substance put on walls and ceilings to make surfaces smooth; *plasterer:* the person who puts the plaster on.
   I'm cold: I'm feeling cold; *It's cold:* the weather is cold.

3 ○ ● **Explanation**   This is a fluency exercise and an opportunity for students to talk about the characters in this episode of the soap.

   ● **Practice**   With the class, discuss what this episode tells us about Archie and Tom. Students should particularly note Archie's pessimism about being able to afford to keep the castle, whereas Tom is optimistic, energetic, practical, and full of ideas. He shows he is not daunted by big problems by the way he immediately sets about mending the boiler, whereas Archie seems a little overwhelmed by all the difficulties. Tom shows himself to be frank and spontaneous against Archie's more measured, controlled personality.

PRACTICE

1 ○ ● **Explanation**   These exercises practise the use of *should/shouldn't* to give advice.

a ● **Practice**   Students were introduced to *should/shouldn't* in the Preview. As a class, students look back at the episode and identify the advice Tom gives Archie, e.g.

You shouldn't sell the house. You should find a way of keeping it.

Students then work in pairs to think of other advice Tom could give Archie, as in the examples. They compare their answers.

A   **Possible answers**
You should replace the heating.
You should find out how to make money.
You shouldn't sell the land.
You should plaster the walls and ceiling.
You should look for the lost treasure.
You should talk to the bank manager.

b ○ ● **Explanation**   Students practise the function of giving advice in this exercise.

● **Practice**   As a class, think of the kind of things you might have problems with, e.g. getting up in the morning, being on time, remembering arrangements, finding time to write letters, etc. Write a list of ideas on the board, then let each student write down, in English, five things they have trouble with. Students work in pairs. One student says what his or her problem is and the other gives advice using *should/shouldn't*, as in the example.

Then they swap roles. Students can role play one dialogue each for the class.

2 ○ ● **Explanation**   This exercise practises the present perfect tense of *have to*, and giving speculative opinions using *perhaps, I expect, probably*, and *maybe*. Students have to put the words in the correct order.

○ ● **Practice**   Students are likely to have problems placing the adverbs, *maybe, probably*, etc. They should look closely at the examples before doing the exercise.

A   1 I expect he's had to use less heating.
2 Maybe he's had to buy a cheaper car.
3 He's probably had to sell valuable things.

4 Perhaps he's had to eat less food.
5 He's probably had to sell some furniture.

3 ○ ● **Explanation**   Students write a formal letter in response to Archie's request for help.

○ ● **Practice**   Read Archie's letter with the students and point out all the features and expressions of formal letter writing.

Features: Address and date in top right-hand corner
Dear *Mr/Mrs* and surname (end with *Yours sincerely,*)
no contractions
clear paragraphing
Expressions: *I am writing to you . . .*
I would be grateful if . . .
I look forward hearing from you.

Then look at the list of people that Archie is going to write to and, as a class, discuss the different ideas each person will have (e.g. the architect may suggest turning the castle into apartments, the pop group manager may suggest turning it into a recording studio). The students, alone or in pairs, choose one person from the list and note down their ideas. Discuss as a class the layout of the reply and put the basic format on the board. Then students write their letters in the class or at home. Collect the letters in and pass them around the class for everyone to read.

4a○ ● **Explanation**   This reading text gives supplementary information. It explains the priest's hole in Archie's castle and provides stimulus for the discussion in **b**.

○ ● **Practice**   Pre-teach vocabulary students may not know: *excitement, seekers, secret, glorious, escape, search, run for home, deadly, version, arrest, torture, willing, traitor, religion.* Read the first paragraph. Students may talk about similar games they played as children. Read the text as a whole. Make sure students understand it.

b ○ ● **Explanation**   This is a free speaking exercise with the emphasis on fluency, not accuracy. The students should concentrate on putting their ideas into English, and not worry about making mistakes.

● **Practice**   The questions can be discussed as a class, or if preferred in small groups first and reported back to the class.

PRONUNCIATION

1 ○ ● **Explanation**   Here is further practice in word stress.

● **Practice**   Say the words aloud together first. Let students practise saying the words with the correct stress.

A   **plas**terer, central **heat**ing, **Cath**olic, **law**yer, have a **look** at, Eliza**beth**an, ex**plo**ded, **val**uable, **an**cestor, il**leg**al, civil **war**, **fur**niture.

2 ○ ● **Explanation**   Students are often unsure when the *-ed* ending makes an extra syllable and when it doesn't. It forms an extra syllable only when the final sound of the main verb is /d/ or /t/. Some students may make the mistake of trying to make three-syllable words of *borrowed, opened, plastered, entered*.

○ ● **Practice**   As a class, make sure students know what a syllable is and how to count them. If necessary, put some familiar words on the board to practise with. Students then work in pairs to complete their columns and they compare their answers as a class.

A   1-syllable: lived, fixed, showed, looked, closed, cleared
2-syllable: borrowed, opened, needed, wanted, plastered, entered

LISTENING

○ ● **Explanation**   This is a listening and reading task. It is a narrative text taken from a work of historical fiction about the escape of King Charles II (son of Charles I, who was beheaded). The king was a very tall man, and he was difficult to disguise.

○ ● **Practice**   Students work as a class or in pairs to try to fill in as many of the gaps as possible. When they have finished, they listen to the tape without the text. They then return to the text to fill in any remaining gaps. They listen again and read the text, correcting their answers and making sure they understand the whole text.

T.3.2
A

There was a sound of running feet, and a *woman's* voice called out, 'Soldiers! Soldiers are *coming!* They are asking what Catholic houses there are here!' Whitgreave went quickly *upstairs* to the king's room. He *opened* the hidden door of the king's wall-cupboard. The king went into the cupboard and climbed down *into* a brick chamber below. Whitegreave *shut* the door and went outside. A few minutes later some horsemen *arrived* in the village. Whitgreave was cutting off the heads of some roses in his *garden*. The soldiers stopped.
'Hey, you there. *Are* you Whitgreave?'
'Why, yes,' said Whitgreave. 'Do you want me?' He opened the gate for them.
'You're a damned Papist,' said the Captain. 'And I'm *certain* you're hiding royalists – maybe King Charles himself!'
Some of the soldiers *told* Whitgreave to get out of the way and went into the house. After a while, the sergeant came back and *said* to the Captain, 'We can't find *anything*.' The Captain was furious, but then told his soldiers to release Whitgreave. Whitgreave went back to his roses. When he knew the soldiers weren't coming back, he went upstairs to *tell* the king. The king came *out* of his secret hiding place.
'I am glad I am not a priest!' he said. 'You *should* put some cushions in that dungeon, Mr Whitgreave. Am I safe?'
'Sir you are!'

READING

1 ○ ● **Explanation**   In this exercise, students must put sentences from a newspaper report in the correct order. The text follows up the story from Episode 3, revealing that one item of the treasure that Archie and Tom discovered has turned out to be very valuable.

○ ● **Practice**   Students can work individually or in pairs. There are various possible solutions, but the final text must make sense. For example, sentence **e**, could be number 2. However, we suggest it should be number 6 because a newspaper report always puts the most interesting events first, and the background information later.

A **Possible answers**

1c Lord Longthorpe has discovered hidden treasure in Longthorpe Castle.

2f An explosion in the castle boiler room blew away part of an old wall, revealing long-lost silver and gold pieces.

3a One of the gold pieces is the King Henry plate.

4g This highly decorated plate was made in Florence in 1532.

5d Experts in London say that its market value is more that £1 million.

6e Lord Longthorpe recently inherited the castle and land from his father.

7h He needs a large sum of money to pay the death duties.

8b Now he can give the plate to the nation to help pay his taxes.

Check questions: *Why is the plate so valuable?*
Will Lord Longthorpe sell it?

2 ○ ● **Practice**   Discuss the different kinds of newspapers in your country. Say which papers in your country would have these kinds of headlines. Before students match the headline to the story, ask them to decide what kind of text it is: serious? humorous? like a magazine article? sensational?

A **Possible answers**

As the text is quite serious and unsensational in tone and style, either of the more serious headings would suit.

Interesting find in thirteenth-century castle or *Civil War treasure found in Castle.*

Options 3

LISTENING

○ ● **Explanation**   This is a short listening exercise with some questions for discussion. Students will not understand everything, but they should understand enough to reach some conclusions.

● **Practice**   Students listen and make deductions using the information on the cassette and possibly the picture too.

A
1 They are at the Tower of London
2 A tour guide is talking.
3 The listeners are tourists.
4 They are sightseeing.
5 *Beefeater, tower,* and *uniform.*

T.3.3 This is the White Tower. These are the famous ravens. It is said that if they ever leave here, England will fall. Now, those gentlemen are Beefeaters. Their red and black uniforms date from the sixteenth century. Now, if you come this way . . . yes, here . . . this green slope is where they executed traitors.
What's that bridge?
That's Tower Bridge.

READING FOR INFORMATION

○ ● **Explanation**   Maps and tourist guides often use symbols or pictographs to indicate an area of particular interest. Some of these are presented here for students to practise with.

a ○ ● **Practice**   Students look at the symbols and try to imagine what they represent. They discuss them as a class to try to reach agreement.

A
1 castle
2 historic house
3 panorama
4 Roman fort

b ● Students study the chart which lists what there is to see and do in the different places and ask and answer each other in pairs, as in the example.
Note   *Castle Howard* is, in fact, a stately home.

SMALL TALK

○ ● **Explanation**   This exercise gives more practice in talking about general subjects with people you don't know very well. It is always acceptable to ask questions about the place where someone lives. Students should also be able to talk about where they live in a competent manner.

a ○ ● **Warm-up**   Ask students to think about how you might describe a town or village: its size/population; why it exists – industry, port, etc; why it is famous (if it is); what's special about it – old buildings, river setting, where something happened in the past; what there is for a visitor to see. Then they read the dialogue to check their answers.

b ● **Practice**   Students work in pairs to prepare their own dialogue. Let them act out their dialogues for the class. If all the places are likely to be known to the class, the place names could be omitted, and the other students have to guess which place is being talked about.

MEASUREMENTS

○ ● **Explanation**   This exercise reminds students how to talk about size and dimensions.

○ ● **Practice**   Make sure students know the adjectives in C. Ask for examples in the class for each, e.g. *I am 1.5m tall. The book is 2cm thick, 12cm wide and 16cm long. The walls are 4m high.* Then ask students to match items from each column to make appropriate sentences.

A
Archie is 1.87m tall.
The walls are 3m thick.
The sitting room is 15m long.
The ceiling in the hall is 10m high.
The castle door is 2.3m wide.

DATES

a ○ ● **Explanation**   Dates are important to understand – especially if you're a tourist. Part **a** practises listening. The students can also write the numbers that they hear, then read them back to you, so that you can check.

● **Practice**   Remind students that dates are generally said as two two-figure numbers (e.g. 1632 – sixteen thirty-two) unless the number is divisible by 100 (e.g. 1500 – fifteen hundred). For the twenty-first

century, we say 'the year two thousand'. Similarly for 2010, we can say two thousand and ten, or twenty ten. Students listen to the dates on the cassette and repeat them. They then try to say the dates that are in their books.

T.3.4 **A**   Nineteen ninety-five, fifteen forty-five, seventeen hundred, twenty twenty, nineteen oh three, nine sixty-seven.

A   Sixteen thirty-two, twelve ninety-five, fifteen hundred, eight twenty, nineteen ninety-nine, two thousand and ten/twenty ten, nineteen oh eight.

b ● Students practise speaking and listening. Each student should think of 4–5 dates, and dictate them to a partner, explaining why the dates are important. The partner then passes on the information to the class.

c ○ ● **Explanation**   The ordinal number is always one above the written number: 1485 = the fifteenth century; 2001 = the twenty-first century.

● **Practice**   You can do this exercise as a class exercise and give the students a few more dates to write up for homework.

A		
1485: 15th century		1890: 19th century
313: 4th century		1701: 18th century
2013: 21st century		1603: 17th century
1066: 11th century		1945: 20th century

FURTHER PRACTICE

○ ● **Explanation**   Students practise using the present perfect and talk about their home/someone else's home.

● **Practice**   Go through the questions quickly with the students, making sure that they understand. Students fill in the questionnaire alone, then ask and answer the questions in pairs. Students can work out a) why the magazine asks these questions and b) what sort of person their partner is, from the answers the partner gives to the questions.

● **Extension**   Students can work in groups to make up their own questionnaires on another subject. Encourage them to use the present perfect when they can. They can then interview students from other groups and report their findings to their group, and to the class.

4
Preview

1 Adverbs (*-ly*)

○ ● **Explanation** Adverbs of manner are words that describe how an action happens or is done, i.e. they describe the verb, and usually come after it in a sentence, e.g. *We sang **loudly*** or *It happened **suddenly***. Regular adverbs are formed by adding *-ly* to an adjective but there are irregular forms that students have to learn. (See the Grammar Summary on page 53.)

a ○ ● **Warm-up** Read the sentences in the table with the class. Look at the column of adverbs and ask:

  What do you think the adverbs do?
  What do you notice about the adverbs?

○ ● **Practice** Read the grammar note under the table and the spelling rules in the Grammar Summary. Ask students to make some other appropriate sentences using the table, e.g. *Sylvia talked carefully. They did the work quickly.*

b ○ ● Read the list of adjectives. Get students to come to the board to write the adverb for each adjective or write them in their books. Students work in pairs to complete the sentences in the table with an appropriate adverb from the list. They compare their answers with the rest of the class.

A	**Possible answers**

Sylvia and Toby spent Toby's prize money
  quickly/easily/carefully.
Archie entered the castle quickly/sadly/happily.
Sylvia sings beautifully/badly/nicely.
Hank left home happily/suddenly/sadly.
Max speaks quickly/clearly/critically.
The balloon climbed gradually/quickly/suddenly.

c ○ ● Read the list of adjectives and irregular adverbs. Note the adverb which changes completely. Ask students to make their own sentences using the adverbs, e.g. *Don't arrive late. They played well.*

d ○ ● Read the paragraph as a class. Make sure students understand all the words. Look at the words in italics one by one. Ask: *Which word does the italicized word describe?* Students must note that adverbs describe verbs and adjectives describe nouns. Do the exercise as a class, making sure everyone understands the correct answers.

○ ● **Extension** Let the students choose two or three of the irregular verbs and ask them to make sentences with the word as an adjective, and then as an adverb. Alternatively, give a student an activity to mime. He or she must do it in a certain manner, and the other students guess what adverb is being described.

A	
early career: adjective	trained *hard*: adverb
good runner: adjective	*hard* worker: adjective
very *fast*: adverb	started *late*: adverb
running *straight*: adverb	*fast* race: adjective
running *well*: adverb	it's a bit *late*: adjective

2 Question tags

○ ● **Explanation** Question tags are used for two main purposes:
  – to get a confirmation of information we have.
  – to ask a question.

They are written in the same way and the only way we know which purpose is meant is by the intonation. So, the way we say them is important. The intonation falls for confirmation, and rises for a question. A lot of intonation practice is required here.

Practice Listen to the sentences on the tape, then listen again and repeat them, copying the intonation. Ask for each sentence: *Does the speaker's intonation rise or fall?* Go through the explanation with the students, making sure they understand, before they go back and mark the intonation pattern on the sentences.

Students mark the question tag with ↗ to show rising intonation for a real question, or ↘ to show falling intonation when asking for agreement or confirmation.

T.4.1
A

Today's a lovely day, isn't it? ↘

You want to come, don't you? ↗

John and I won't need an umbrella, will we? ↘

Henry loves hot weather, doesn't he? ↘

You can drive us there, can't you? ↗

Edna's got a picnic lunch, hasn't she? ↗

Edna and Henry don't like swimming, do they? ↘

The ice-cream hasn't melted, has it? ↗

The car isn't working, is it? ↘

b **Explanation** These questions are to draw the students' attention to the grammar rules involved in making question tags.

Practice Do this exercise as a class. The students can work out the rules for themselves and then check them with the Grammar Summary on page 53.

A

1 **Positive main sentence:**	**Negative (-) question tag:**
Today's a lovely day,	isn't it?
You want to come,	don't you?
Henry loves hot weather,	doesn't he?
You can drive us there,	can't you?
Edna's got a picnic lunch,	hasn't she?
2 **Negative main sentence:**	**Positive (+) question tag:**
John and I won't need an umbrella,	will we?
Edna and Henry don't like swimming,	do they?
The ice-cream hasn't melted,	has it?
The car isn't working,	is it?

3 You only repeat the auxiliary in the question tag: is/isn't, do/don't, does/doesn't, can/can't, has/hasn't, will/won't, have/haven't.

4 The pronoun in the question tag agrees with the subject in the main sentence.

5 Yes, it is.

c Students work in pairs to write the question tags. They listen to the tape in order to check their answers and practise the correct intonation. They mark the question tags with an intonation arrow to show if it rises or falls.

T.4.2
A

1 They want to go to the beach, don't they? ↘

2 James can't swim, can he? ↗

3 I can stay on the beach, can't I? ↗

4 We've got some sun cream somewhere, haven't we? ↗

5 Edna's very brown, isn't she? ↗

6 Henry and Edna'll look after our things, won't they? ↘

7 Lunch is at twelve, isn't it? ↗

8 People shouldn't swim after a heavy meal, should they? ↘

d Students have to match a main sentence from column **A** with the right question tag from column **B**. Before they start, ask: *What are the main rules about tags?* Students can work alone or in pairs to do the exercise once they are clear what they have to do. They should check their answers with the class.

A

A	B
The weather isn't nice today,	is it?
I'm going this week,	aren't I?
You don't want this,	do you?
Archie drives too fast,	doesn't he?
They enjoyed their holiday,	didn't they?
We've nearly finished,	haven't we?
Rita will win the race,	won't she?
Hank can play the clarinet,	can't he?
Poppy should be nicer to Max,	shouldn't she?
Tom didn't mend the boiler,	did he?

3 *wants(s) to do want(s) somebody to do*

Explanation Students often make mistakes with *want* in English because other languages formulate it differently, e.g. I want *that* you do something. Therefore, practice is needed to get the grammatical construction right. Students need to know the difference between:

I want to paint the bathroom. (I want to do the job myself.)
I want an expert to paint the bathroom. (I want someone else to do the job.)

Practice Look at the pictures and read the example sentences. Ask:

What does/doesn't Sally/Dad/Mum/Tom/the dog/the cat want to do?
What does Dad want Sally to do?
What does Mum want Tom to do?

Students work in pairs to make a list of what each person in the picture wants to do and what they want another person in the picture to do. Compare answers as a class.

A **Possible answers**
Dad doesn't want Sally to play.
Dad wants to go fishing.
Mum wants Tom to wash his hands.
Mum wants to sit down with a book.
Mum doesn't want Tom to play football.
Tom wants to play football.
The cat wants to eat.
The cat wants Mum to feed it.
The dog wants to go for a walk.
The dog wants Dad to take it for a walk.

● Then students work in groups. Each student says what he or she wants to do in the evening or at the weekends and one thing he or she wants someone else to do (see example). Students report back to the class what one person in his or her group wants to do and what that person wants someone else to do, e.g.
. . . wants to go away for the weekend. He/She wants his/her parents to lend him/her the car.

4 Present perfect with time phrases

a ○ ● **Explanation** This exercise revises the differences between the past simple and the present perfect and introduces time phrases which can go with the present perfect. Time phrases that fix an event in the past must go with the past simple and *not* the present perfect, as in the first two example dialogues. Time phrases that continue into the present go with the present perfect, as in the third example dialogue.

○ ● **Practice** Read the three dialogues and discuss the time phrases. Ask: *Does it refer to a time that is completely in the past, or does it include the present? What tense is used with the time phrase?*

b ○ Students compare these dialogues to their own language, to see if their language makes a difference between the two tenses or not. Then ask them if they can think of other time phrases which include the present, e.g. *this week, this month, until now, these days.*

c ○ Students translate the three dialogues into their own languages.

5 Present perfect with *for* and *since*

○ ● **Presentation** In Unit 2 we learnt the difference between *for* and *since*. Here students practise expressing a period of time by using *since*, i.e. from the point the period began, instead of using *for* which describes the length of the period of time.

● **Practice** Read the example and do the first one as a class so students know what they have to do. They should calculate their answers with the actual date/time as 'now'. The example and answers below use 1991 as now. Students work in pairs to work out the dates first, then ask them to give the sentences orally round the class for the first few examples. Ask the pairs to pick one or two of the remaining characters to write about at home. Give the students only as much practice as you think they need, as it is a long exercise.

A **Sample answers**
Anna has been a doctor since *1987.*
Archie hasn't raced since *1990* when he broke his legs. He has been Lord Longthorpe since *1990*, too.
Hank has lived with his father since *1986*. He has been at university since *1989*. He has been a law student since *1990.*
Max has lived in Lion Place since *1981*. He has been married to Poppy since *1990*. He has been the owner of Lion Enterprises since *1979*, and has been in England since *1974.*

---

6 Past participles

○ ● **Explanation**   These are regular and irregular past participles. Students should check their answers in their dictionary.

○ ● **Practice**   Students work in pairs to find the answers and check them as a class.

A

worked	come	seen
won	got	transferred
run	played	cut
begun	studied	gone
been	taken	spent
had	told	learnt
grown up	stuck	left

7 Vocabulary

○ ● **Presentation**   This is an activity to sort words into two main categories, *sports* and *education*, with a third group for words that do not fit into either of these categories.

○ ● **Practice**   Students need to check that they understand all the words. Then they work in small groups to sort them into the appropriate groups. They compare their lists with other groups.

A

Sports	Education	Other words
jogging	exam	band
fit	term	furious
fitness	fail	grow up
race	college	conservation
trainer	degree	successful
train	allowance	clarinet
exercise		lawyer
champion		

The inside track

T.4.3   Hank meets Rita at the sports centre. He is surprised to see her there; he did not know she was a top-class athlete. He is there to talk to the manager about a concert for his band. When Rita's training session has finished, they talk again. Hank tells Rita that he has failed his exams. He does not want to be a lawyer, he wants to change universities and study conservation. He knows Max will not approve, but Rita advises him to discuss it with his father. Hank gives Rita a lift back to Lion Place. Max is there. Hank tells him about failing his exams, and his plans. Max points out that Hank has only lived in cities and does not know anything about the countryside. He makes Hank an offer: if he works outdoors for a year, then he will help him.

The people in this episode

Rita is relaxed and confident. She is modest about her running, and turns the conversation away from the subject, leaving Hank to talk about himself. She has a more realistic attitude than Hank, and gives him good advice.

Hank feels sorry for himself. He is worried about telling his father that he has failed his exams and wants to change his course. In the end he does, encouraged by Rita's sensible advice. Max's obvious contempt makes him angry, and helps him to assert himself – probably for the first time.

Max treats Hank like a child rather than an adult. His reaction to Hank's plans is realistic, but not very good for the father – son relationship. He is not entirely negative, however, and does offer Hank a condition for supporting his plan.

● **Warm-up**   Look at the picture. Ask:

Why is Rita dressed like that?
Why are she and Hank there?
Has Hank just arrived, or is he just leaving?
Are Hank and his father talking about the weather?
Are they discussing politics?
Are they happy in each other's company?

Play the cassette of the whole episode. Then play the cassette section by section. Ask what is happening in each section, where the characters are, what they are doing, what they are talking about. Is there a key point in the episode when something/someone changes?

Check questions:
Why are Rita and Hank at the sports centre?
Is Rita good at sport? Is Hank good at law?
What is Hank's problem?
What does Hank tell Max?
What is Max's reaction?

Performance 4

COMPREHENSION

○ ● **Explanation** These are quick comprehension questions. Do not spend too long on them.

○ ● **Practice** Read all the statements through once. Four of the statements (4,6,8,11) are correct. Students must identify the statements that are wrong and correct them.

> **A**
> 1 No, he meets her at the sports centre.
> 2 No, she trains in the evenings and at weekends.
> 3 No, Hank has come to talk to the manager.
> 5 No, Max doesn't know about Rita's running.
> 7 No, Max thinks Hank should be a lawyer. Hank wants to work outdoors.
> 9 No, he's going back to study conservation.
> 10 No, he doesn't have time for it.
> 12 No, Max says that Hank doesn't know about the countryside. When he has worked in the country for a year, he will help him.

PRACTICE

1 ○ ● **Explanation** This exercise practises the use of question tags. It checks students' comprehension of the sentences. It also shows how, by changing the verbs, we turn the sentence from positive to negative, or negative to positive. It prepares students for the next exercise.

○ ● **Practice** Remind students that the verb in the main sentence and the verb in the tag must be positive/negative or negative/positive. Read the example together. Let the students do the exercise in pairs and then as a class.

> **A**
> 1a; You don't have to work hard, do you?
> 2b; You will tell him, won't you?
> 3a; You can't retake your exams, can you?

2 ○ ● **Explanation** In this exercise, students practise producing question tags, using information from the text. The resulting sentences are all slightly critical comments on what someone has said, without being rude.

○ ● **Practice** Students should try this exercise in pairs. They can check their answers with the rest of the class.

> **A**
> 1 You went to/were at a nightclub last night, didn't you/weren't you?
> You haven't worked very hard, have you?
> It's too difficult, isn't it?
> 2 He's lazy, isn't he?
> He doesn't finish anything, does he?
> 3 You won't sell it, will you?
> 4 You want to be a GP, don't you?
> 5 You could get married, couldn't you?

3 ○ ● **Explanation** In this exercise, students have to distinguish between *want to* and *want someone to*. They work through a list to decide which things Rita wants to do, which things her trainer wants her to do, and which they both want Rita to do.

○ ● **Practice** Students make three columns, one headed: *Rita wants to . . .*, the second headed: *Rita and her trainer want her to . . .*, and the third headed: *Rita's trainer wants her to . . ..* They then work in pairs to read the list of things and complete their columns. As a class, students should take turns to read out one full sentence from their columns.

> **A**
> *Rita wants to:*
> get promotion at work; buy some new red shorts.
>
> *Rita and her trainer want her to:*
> get a place in the Olympic team; win a gold medal; break the world record.
>
> *Rita's trainer wants her to:*
> do a six-mile run every morning; run 100 metres, then stop, then run 100 metres; do weight-lifting for half an hour a day; think positively; eat more carbohydrates.

4 ○ ● **Explanation** Students are introduced here to key vocabulary for exercise 5. It is a simple matching exercise. Students may use their dictionaries if they need to.

○ ● **Practice** Students can do this exercise alone or in pairs, before checking as a class. Make sure they can pronounce the words correctly.

> **A**
>
> | polar bear 4 | aerial 8 | glacier 2 | chart 3 |
> | hills 6 | ridge 7 | tent 5 | camp 1 |

5/6

○ ● **Explanation** This is a listening task. The words to be filled in the gaps are all verbs. This text shows how the present simple and continuous, present perfect and past simple are used within a single sequence of conversations.

○ ● **Practice** Let students listen to the cassette first. Then they work in pairs and try to fill in the gaps by working out the answers and remembering what they can. They can listen to the tape again to check their answers. Discuss any differences in class.

T.4.4	**Base Camp**	Prudence, where are you now?
A	**Prudence**	*I've passed* Dickens Glacier. Now I'*m walking* south of the Bleak Hills.
	Sylvia	I'm afraid they've lost contact for the moment . . .
		(Days later)
	Base Camp	Hello. Prudence. Can you *hear* me?
	Prudence	Yes.
	Base Camp	Where *are* you now?
	Prudence	*I've left* the area of the Bleak Hills, and I'*m crossing* Marley Ridge. *I've lost* one of my radio aerials. I *slept* at Oliver's Camp last night, and there *was* a strong wind. It *blew* away my tent. Everything *has gone*.
	Base Camp	Prudence, where are you? Can we *have* your position please?
	Prudence	I can't tell you. *I've lost* my charts.
	Base Camp	Prudence, can you *see* the plane? Repeat, can you *see* the plane?
	Prudence	I *can't see* the plane yet. But I think I *can hear* some polar bears . . .
	Hal	Polar bears! There aren't any polar bears in the Antarctic!
	Prudence	I can see a plane! It'*s flying* low. The plane *has landed*! Thank goodness!
	Sylvia	She's OK. She's made it!

7 ○ ● **Explanation** This is a writing task, based on the listening text in exercise **5**. Remind students that the present perfect in the listening exercise will usually change into past simple in a written report of the events. However, students should use their own words, and not keep too closely to the original words.

○ ● **Practice** Read the example beginning. Students can choose their own dates but the tenses here will help them start correctly. Let students work in their groups to pick out the important information for their report. They should also refer to the chart. They write the report and then read it out as a news item to the class, or they can jot down the main ideas as a group and write the rest for homework. Then they can read each other's to compare.

PRONUNCIATION

1a ○ ● **Explanation** Here is practice in sentence stress. Students should try to work out the answers for themselves.

○ ● **Practice** Students read the sentences, then let them listen to the sentences in context by playing the first section of Episode 4 to them. Students work in pairs to try to find the main stress in each sentence. Then play the cassette for students to check their answers. You may have to play the tape a few times, as sometimes students have difficulty in hearing where the stress is.

T.4.5	1 Has your term **fin**ished?
A	2 Yes, we finished last **Fri**day.
	3 I've been in **Lon**don since then.
	4 What **kind** of training do you do?
	5 Do **you** run?
	6 No, I don't have **time** for exercise.
	7 I suppose **not**.
	8 You have to work **hard** at college, don't you?
	9 See you **later**, Hank.

b ● Students work in pairs. They practise the dialogue in the first part of Episode 4, paying special attention to intonation and stress. Let some of the pairs act out their dialogue for the class.

2 ○ ● **Explanation** The exercise practises the different ways of pronouncing 'a' in a word. Students must match the spelling to the correct sound. They should choose the sound that is made in context, not when the word is spoken by itself out of context, e.g. in the first example *a* is listed under /ə/ not under /æ/ because that is how it is pronounced in a sentence.

- **Practice**   Students work in pairs. They make a list of all the words with an 'a' in the first part of Episode 4. Read the sounds with their examples to remind students. They continue to work in pairs to put the words with the right sound. There is one word with an 'a' in it whose sound is not represented here. Ask the students to identify it.

/ə/ has, are, Rita, at, and, a, man*a*ger
/æ/ Hank, that, exactly, have, band, m*a*nager
/ɑː/ hard, last
/ɒ/ what, want
/eɪ/ Friday (can be /ɪ/), train, play, place, later

There is also the long /ɔː/ vowel in talk.

3 ○ ● **Explanation**   Here is another exercise matching spelling and sound. Students who tend to prefer American pronunciation may have different answers.

- **Practice**   Students work in pairs. Partners say the words to each other and decide if the pairs rhyme or not. They compare their answers as a class.

Note To rhyme in English, the last syllables must have matching vowels *and* final consonants.

Non-rhyming pairs: Can't/want, watch/catch, crashed/fast (different vowels or consonants).

Note Sometimes the vowel in *more* is a diphthong, and therefore different from *law*, where it is a single sound.

READING

1 ○ ● **Explanation**   This task involves sorting out muddled information so that it makes sense.

○ ● **Warm-up**   Students work in small groups to read the headings and make sure they know what kind of information goes with each heading.

○ ● **Practice**   In their groups, they read through the information in each category, moving the inappropriate information to the correct section. They compare answers with other groups.

Curriculum Vitae
Hank Jefferson
Lion House
3 Lion Place
Richmond, Surrey

Age 21

Education
St Olave's Primary School
Ledchester College
University of London

Academic achievements
GCSE: French (B), English (C), Maths (A), Music (C), Chemistry (D), History (B), Geography (A), Computer Studies (B)
A Levels: Maths (B), Economics (B), French (C)

Other skills
Knowledge of IBM computers, typing, clean driving licence, good rider (horses), play the clarinet (Grade 7), own a motorbike

Work experience
Holiday job as courier with travel firm
Temporary ranger in Snowdonia National Park
Restaurant work as a student

Hobbies and interests
Outdoor work, skiing, walking, *jazz, football*

Health
Good

2 ○ ● **Explanation**   Students use their answer for exercise **1** to write their own CV.

○ ● **Warm-up**   Before they begin this writing task, ask students:

Would you use the same categories as Hank did in his CV?
If not, what would you use?
Would you present the information in this order?
Would Hank write the same CV for entry to an educational course as he would for a job?
How might it be different?

- **Practice**   Students write their own CV based on the discussion and Hank's CV.

- **Extension**   Students imagine they are applying for a course or a job. They send their CV to the institution and write a covering letter based on Hank's. Remind students of the format conventions for letter writing. This can be done as homework.

Options 4

GRAMMAR

○ ● **Explanation**   Verbs are often used as nouns in the *-ing* form. These forms are called gerunds or verbal nouns. Students need practice in recognizing grammatical functions from the position of the word. This will be less of a problem for students who have a knowledge of the grammar of their own languages.

○ ● **Practice**   Do the first few sentences with the class, unless your class is used to doing this kind of exercise in their own language. Ask appropriate leading questions:

Which word or words does the underlined word go with?
What function does this word have in the sentence?
What kind of word describes a noun?
What kind of word describes a verb?

When they understand what to do, students can work alone or in pairs to finish the exercise. They compare their answers with other students.

A   *jogging:* noun
keep fit: verb
keep-fit: adjective; *train:* verb; *hard:* adverb
running: noun; *hard:* adjective
fast: adverb
running: noun; *slowly:* adverb
running: verb; *race:* noun
swimming: noun; *best:* adjective; *exercise:* noun
(*swimming* in *going swimming* is part of a verb)
swim: verb; *well:* adverb
true: adjective

○ ● **Extension**   In the exercise above, students will have realized that we can use words in different forms: the *-ing* form, e.g. *swimming* can be used as a verb, e.g. *I'm swimming* or *She's swimming fast*; as a noun, e.g. *Swimming is fun*, or as an adjective, e.g. *a swimming race*. A word like *fast* can be used as an adjective, e.g. *a fast race* or as an adverb, e.g. *he swims fast*. Ask students to make their own sentences with the same word showing two or three different uses.

PUZZLE

○ ● **Explanation**   Adverbs of manner go after the direct object in English. This exercise practises putting the adverb or adverbial phrase in the right position after the direct object.

A   I did my exams very badly.
Max always takes work seriously.
You have to work hard at college, don't you?
You'll shut the door quietly, won't you?
She won her race easily, didn't she?

FURTHER PRACTICE

○ ● **Explanation**   This gives students an opportunity to practise the grammar and intonation of question tags.

● **Practice**   Students must work in pairs. They each work alone to consider what they know and what they need to find out about their partner. They should prepare the two sets of questions separately to ensure they get the intonation right. Then they ask and answer the questions. Ask some students to role play a few of their questions for the class.

VOCABULARY

○ ● **Explanation**   This is a spelling exercise for words ending in *-er* or *-or*. Students make words by choosing a beginning, middle, and end from each column. All are jobs except one – *ancestor*.

A   manager   editor   reporter   doctor   trainer
builder   ancestor   director   actor   lawyer
plumber

LISTENING

○ ● **Explanation**   In this exercise students have to listen intensively in order to cross-check written and listening texts.

● **Practice**   Students listen to the interview. They consult the text and try to remember where the notes are wrong and correct them. They then listen to the interview again while checking the notes and mark where they are wrong with the correct information. They can listen again to check their answers.

A He's been at university for two years, not three.
He failed his second year exam, not his third year exam.
The university would allow him to resit the exam, but he doesn't want to.
He's not studying physics but law.
He doesn't want to be a lawyer. His father wants him to be a lawyer.
He wants to study conservation, which he can't do at his present university. That is why he wants to change universities.
The university can give credit for work he's done so far. In any case, he's studied law.
They have a lot of people doing the course, and so they can't offer a place straight away.

T.4.6

A

Professor		You've completed two years at university?
Hank		Yes, that's right.
Professor		And you passed your first year exams?
Hank		Yes, but I failed my second year exams.
Professor		Can you repeat the year? Does the university allow students to resit exams?
Hank		Yes, I can repeat the year if I want, but I don't want to.
Professor		I see. You're studying law?
Hank		Yes.
Professor		Do you want to be a lawyer?
Hank		No, I don't. My father wants me to be a lawyer.
Professor		Can you change subjects at your present university?
Hank		Some people do, but I want to study conservation, and there isn't a course.
Professor		We have a course in Conservation Studies, as you know. We could give you credit for the work you've already done for your degree, I think. We like our students to know something about law.
Hank		That's good.
Professor		Yes, but first you have to gain a place. We have a lot of people wanting to take this course.

ENRICHMENT

○ ● **Explanation**   This is an oral exercise. Students practise using *must be/can't be* to describe their conclusions about something. We use *must be* when we are making a strong guess about something. *Can't be* is the negative (not *mustn't be*).

● **Practice**   Students study the picture and example sentences. Then they can make a few more conclusions about the picture, e.g. *They must be asleep.*

Students study the picture on page 46 in pairs and discuss what each of the characters must be feeling and why, using the words given to help them.

A   **Possible answers**
They can't be in. The car's not there./There's a newspaper and milk on the doorstep.
They must be in. There's smoke coming from the chimney./I can hear music./I can see the dog upstairs.

Picture on page 46:
Sally can't be hungry. She's not eating her food.
Dad must be irritated, because she won't eat.
Mum must be tired, because she wants to sit down and relax.
Tom can't be tired, because he wants to continue playing football.
The cat must be hungry. It wants to eat.
The dog must be unhappy. It wants to go for a walk.

5
Preview

1 First conditional

a ○ ● **Explanation** Students are introduced to the first conditional through Sandra, who is playing a board game called 'Snakes and Ladders'. The first conditional is used to talk about the result of a possible future action (referred to as a condition). The condition is expressed in the *if* clause using the present tense. The result clause is in the future tense.

○ ● **Warm-up** Ask the students to look at the game, read the sentences and find out how the game is played, first of all. (You go up the ladders and down the snakes.)

○ ● **Practice** Students study the 'Snakes and Ladders' board that Sandra is playing on, and read the sentences. They answer the first two questions.

A
1 No, she hasn't thrown the dice yet, she is still thinking, but she is going to throw the dice.
2 The numbers which will be good for her are:
   2 because she'll go up the ladder to square seventy-three.
   3 because she'll move on to square thirty-six.
   5 because she'll go up the ladder to square sixty-six.

Now students look at Sandra's thoughts and underline the verbs. Two tenses are used: the future and the present. Ask students the next two questions. Emphasize that in order to express a possibility in the future, the *if* clause is always in the present and the result is always in the future tense.

Note If students look at the condition clauses they can see that the conditions are all possible (she could throw any number), but not certain. The result clauses are all certain to happen, if their conditions are fulfilled.

b ○ ● **Explanation** This is an ordering exercise which enables the students to practise the first conditional.

● **Practice** Read the list of stages. Make sure students understand the action verbs: *type, stick on, photocopy, fold*. Students work in pairs to decide on the logical order for each stage. Check their answers.

c ● Students in pairs make sentences about who should do which job. Read the example to give students a model. Students can do the exercise orally in pairs before you check their answers.

2 Reflexive verbs and pronouns

a ○ ● **Explanation** There are not many common reflexive verbs in English, e.g. *to enjoy yourself*, but reflexive pronouns are used when the same person is subject and object, e.g. *I treated myself to a new skirt*. (Not *I treated me to a new skirt*.) (See the Grammar Summary on page 63.)

○ ● **Warm-up** Discuss examples of the reflexive in the students' own language. Identify the English pronoun form by drawing the students' attention to the example in the table.

○ ● **Practice** Students read the text in class, first for meaning, then to identify the reflexive pronouns. Then they work in pairs to complete the table with the singular and plural forms of the reflexive pronouns. Ask: *Why are there two forms for the third person singular?* Students compare their answers as a class.

A

	Singular	Plural
First person	myself	ourselves
Second person	yourself	yourselves
Third person	himself (masc.)	themselves
	herself (fem.)	

b ○ ● Answer these questions as a class exercise.

c ○ Students translate the first paragraph in order to compare the use of the reflexive in their own language and in English.

3   Vocabulary

○ ● **Explanation**   Students are introduced to some of the new vocabulary in Episode 5. They will need to use a dictionary to help them classify the words into three groups.

○ ● **Practice**   Students work in pairs to discuss the words and put them under the correct heading. They compare their lists in class and check that they can pronounce them correctly.

A	Medical	To do with work	To do with food
	consultant	earn	menu
	hospital	freelance	meal
	casualty	inefficient	mushroom
	GP	job	waiter
	doctor	project	garlic

Food for thought

T.5.1 Anna and Toby are at home in Lion Place. There is no food and they are both too tired to go to the supermarket or cook. They decide to go out for a meal instead. They choose 'Brother Sun', where they can eat outside. They order their meal and drinks, and then talk about their plans for the future while they wait for their food. Anna is thinking about going into general practice rather than being a hospital doctor. Toby wants to specialize in building conversion, either for a firm, or for himself. They have just started their meal, and are talking about how relaxed they are feeling, especially with Suzi in Spain, when Suzi bursts on the scene. She has a man with her, who Suzi describes as a film director who is going to give her a part in a film in America.

The people in this episode

Anna and **Toby** are 'off duty' here. They are obviously good friends and both find it relaxing to be with each other. You can tell from the way they talk about their plans that they do not often get an opportunity to talk together like this. They probably do not have time with Anna's hours of hospital work. They also do not have Suzi to worry about (until she turns up again, having apparently met a man on the plane).

Suzi is as exuberant as ever, full of bounce and enthusiasm. She has lots of confidence, and is quite happy to interrupt her brother and sister's peaceful meal.

● **Warm-up**   Look at the picture. Ask:

Who is in it?
Where are they?
What are they doing?
What do you think is happening?

Play the cassette.

Who is having dinner?
What is the name of the restaurant?
Why is Suzi there?

Play the cassette again, section by section. Ask the students what has happened in each section. Ask questions like these:

Why are Anna and Toby going to eat out?
What do they order?
What do Anna and Toby want to do in the future?
Are they expecting Suzi? Who is she with?

Performance 5

COMPREHENSION

1 ○ ● **Explanation**   These questions ask students to check points of detail in the text. Some questions need a full answer. In others, the answers can be one or two words.

● **Practice**   Read the questions together and discuss the answers as a class.

A   1 They haven't got anything to eat.
2 Nobody
3 Toby
4 They eat at Brother Sun at nine o'clock.
5 They order drinks (wine and whisky) and the special, fish, with garlic mushrooms and pasta with cream to start.

41

6 Anna wants to be a GP.
7 Toby wants to do conversions, either with a company or possibly work for himself.
8 Because Toby doesn't like working for other people.
9 No, he was inefficient.
10 She's been to Spain.
11 Lucas, a film director Suzi met on the plane.

2 ○ ● **Explanation** This exercise checks the students' overall understanding of the text. It also gives them practice in the use of gerunds.

● **Practice** Let students look at the subjects themselves or in pairs first, before checking the answers orally with the class.

A They talk about: going to the supermarket.
cooking.
paying for things.
working hard.
moving to a different job.
working for other people.
They don't talk about: moving to a different country.
working in an office.

Extra subjects They also talk about where they're going to eat, what they're going to order, getting married, Suzi.

3 ○ ● **Explanation** This is an oral fluency exercise on the students' understanding of the characters. Ask them to give reasons for their answers from the text.

● **Practice** Students work in small groups to discuss the statements.

A **Possible answers**
1 Yes, they find it easy to talk and be with one another.
2 No, but he's getting well paid for the job he's doing at the moment.
3 Not very. If she were ambitious, she would probably want to specialize rather than be a GP.
4 Not very. He prefers to work on smaller projects.
5 No, she does like it, but it's obviously tiring.
6 Toby likes Max, but he doesn't like working for him.
7 Yes. She's full of energy, enthusiasm, self-confidence, and determination.
8 No. She knows what she wants to do with her life and finds ways to get what she wants.

PRACTICE

1 ○ ● **Explanation** Students practise conditional sentences, using *if* and *will*. They are given the *if*-clause and must complete the second half of each sentence with *will*.

○ ● **Practice** Students work in pairs to complete the sentences. They can refer to the text for who the speaker is but they will have to work out the structure themselves.

A 1 If we go to Brother Sun, we'll sit outside. (Anna).
2 If you book for nine, I'll have time for a shower. (Anna).
3 If they haven't got white wine, I'll have red wine. (Anna).
4 If there isn't any fish, we'll eat chicken. (Anna and Toby).
5 If I leave the hospital, I'll become a GP. (Anna).
6 If Johnson & Lewis don't offer me a job, I'll work for myself. (Toby).

2 ○ ● **Explanation** Here is more practice in conditional sentences with *if* and *will*, this time completing the verb in both parts of the sentence.

○ ● **Practice** Students can do the exercise in pairs and check their answers with the rest of the class.

A 1 **Waiter** If you *aren't* here by nine, we *won't hold* the table.
2 **Anna** If you *pay* for the meal, I *won't* come.
3 **Anna** If we *sit* outside, we*'ll get* cold.
4 **Toby** If Johnson & Lewis *do* conversions, I*'ll ask* them for a job.

(All of the sentences are slightly different from what they said in the story.)

3 ○ ● **Explanation** This translation exercise gives further practice with conditional sentences containing *if* and *will*, and the opportunity for students to compare the two languages.

Note *Can* is also used in the main clause, referring to future time: *If I ever get married, I can still work as a GP.*

○ **Practice** Students work in pairs or alone to translate the sentences. The sentence that does not refer to future time is: *It's more difficult to do hospital work if you have a family.* We call this form of conditional a 'time-free' or 'zero' conditional.

4a○ ● **Explanation**   This an exercise to practise reflexive pronouns. Reflexive pronouns are much less widely used in English than in many other languages, and each expression should be learnt as an item of vocabulary:

cut oneself, enjoy oneself, look at oneself in the mirror, treat oneself, make oneself comfortable, make oneself something, help oneself (to) something, buy oneself something

○ ● **Practice**   Students work in pairs to match the phrases in **A** with those from **B**. They read and compare their answers as a class.

A							
1e	2f	3b	4g	5c	6a	7h	8d

b ○ ● **Explanation**   Students describe their morning routine using verbs that are reflexive in many other languages, but are not reflexive in English: *shave, wash, get up, comb one's hair, get dressed, get ready.*

● **Practice**   First make sure that students have the necessary vocabulary. Students work alone for three minutes to write a description of their morning routine.

c ● They compare their description with their partner's to find out if they do things in the same order or not. One partner from each pair can tell the class what the differences are.

5a○ ● **Explanation**   This is a recording of people talking about their work, with a listening task for students.

● **Practice**   Play the interview with Ann through once while the students listen. They should pay particular attention to the points listed in the table. Then students fill in the table with as much information as they can remember. Play the cassette for a second and third time if necessary for students to check their answers. Let them check with each other, too. Repeat for the second interview.

● **Extension**   Students work in pairs to make their own interviews about their own jobs using the list of details as prompts for the questions. They can act out the interview for the class, or make a recording to play to the class.

A		Interview 1	Interview 2
Name of job		Nurse	Waiter
Interesting		Yes	No
Long hours		Yes	Yes
Hard work		Yes	Yes
Well paid		No	Yes
Work for yourself		No	No
Meet interesting people		Sometimes	Sometimes
Sit at a desk		No	No

T.5.2	**1** Interviewer	What do you do?

1 Interviewer   What do you do?
Ann   I'm a nurse. I'm senior theatre sister at the Infirmary.
Interviewer   That's a difficult job, isn't it?
Ann   No, not really. I've trained for it, and I know what to do. But it is a responsible job. I mean, I sometimes think, 'this person's life depends on all of us getting things right'.
Interviewer   Is it hard work? Do you work long hours?
Ann   It is hard work, yes. In the theatre, you're on your feet all the time. You can be there for six hours without a break. That's tough. The hours per week aren't long, though. I work four days on, three days off. It's about 38 hours, I suppose.
Interviewer   Is it well paid?
Ann   It isn't bad now. But nobody goes into nursing for the money, do they? No, it isn't well paid, really. I don't mind, though. I love it.
Interviewer   Who employs you? The health authority or the hospital?
Ann   The hospital.
Interviewer   Do you like the people you work with? Do you meet interesting people?
Ann   Some people think doctors are interesting, but I don't think so. Surgeons are very self-centred, I find. I met interesting people when I worked on the wards, but my patients now are usually unconscious!

2 Interviewer Ferdie, you're a waiter, aren't you?

Ferdie That's right.

Interviewer Is it an interesting job?

Ferdie No, not really. I'm working as a waiter to earn money for college.

Interviewer Is it hard work? Do you work long hours?

Ferdie Yes, it's very hard work. I work perhaps 60 or 70 hours a week.

Interviewer Those are very long hours. Do you always have to work those hours?

Ferdie No, just when the work is there, in the tourist season, I need to do it. Then I can earn a lot of money. You don't earn so much in the winter.

Interviewer Who do you work for?

Ferdie I work in a big restaurant in the centre. The people who own it are cousins of mine.

Interviewer What do you want to do when you finish at college?

Ferdie A desk job!

Interviewer Do you meet interesting people in your job?

Ferdie Yes, I do, sometimes.

Interviewer What's the worst thing about the job? Is it the hours, or being on your feet all day?

Ferdie No, the worst thing is that I don't enjoy food any more. You don't when you're working with it all day!

b ○ ● **Explanation** This exercise gives students a chance to recycle language from the listening text.

○ ● **Practice** Students work in small groups of three or four to write sentences like the examples, using the information from their table in **a**.

c ○ ● **Explanation** This exercise offers optional further practice on the listening and can be treated as a freer oral exercise.

● **Practice** Students can work in their small groups to discuss what else was in the interview but not in the table. For example, the interviewer asks Ann if her job is difficult and Ann talks about that; Ferdie talks about why he works such long hours. Students should try to remember these details. Play the

cassette again after you have heard their answers so they can check how much they have remembered.

6a ○ ● **Explanation** This is a discussion, followed by practice of time-free conditionals, in which both parts of the sentence are in the present simple.

● **Practice** Students work in pairs to list the good and bad things about each job. As a class, students discuss their opinions on the advantages and disadvantages of being a GP or a hospital doctor.

b ○ ● Again in their pairs, students write sentences using time-free conditionals to describe things that are generally true about these two kinds of doctors. Students compare their sentences as a class.

c ○ ● **Explanation** This is an extension exercise giving practice in describing jobs. Students do not have to use conditional sentences all the time.

● **Practice** Students work in groups. Each group decides on a particular kind of job and makes a list of the good and bad points without saying what it is. As a class, each group describes their job to the rest of the students, who can ask questions to work out what the job is.

d ● Students describe their own jobs or the job they would like to have. They work alone to list the good and bad points. Then they describe it to a partner or to the class. Alternatively, they can write about their job for homework.

PRONUNCIATION

1 ○ ● **Explanation** Here is further practice in word stress.

● **Practice** Say the words aloud in class, then let students write the answers down individually from memory. Alternatively, students work out the main stress first in pairs, then say the words aloud to them so they can correct their mistakes. Practise the pronunciation with the class.

| **A** | **su**permarket, **hos**pital, ine**ffi**cient, **free**lance, con**sul**tant, en**joy** yourself, ex**haus**ted, **diffi**cult, **pro**ject, de**part**ment, con**ver**sion, I**tal**ian |

2 ○ ● **Explanation** Students listen for sentence stress.

● **Practice** Students listen and write down the word that they think is stressed in each sentence. Play the cassette a second time for students to check their answers. Discuss the sentences where we would normally stress a different word.

T.5.3

A

a We'll have to go to the **supermarket**.
b **I'll** buy the wine.
c Is nine o'clock all **right**?
d The **special** looks good.
e I think I want to be a **GP**.
f You have to think about the **future**.
g It's **much** better to work for yourself.
h There was a **card** from her today.

3 ○ ● **Explanation** Having met phonetic symbols in Book 1, students now need practice at recognizing the vowel symbols, as these are generally used in dictionaries. In this exercise, we practise /iː/, /e/, /ɜː/, /ɪə/.

○ ● **Warm-up** Write the four symbols on the board. Ask students for a word that contains each sound. Write an example under each symbol.

○ ● **Practice** Students work in pairs. They list the words for each sound. Compare answers as a class. Students can also use their dictionaries to check their answers.

A

/iː/	evening, treat, feel, meal, scenic, please, peaceful
/e/	head, menu, said
/ɜː/	earn, learn, conversion
/ɪə/	idea, ser-ious, here

READING

1 ○ ● **Explanation** Students read for information.

○ ● **Warm-up** Study the advertisements in pairs or as a class. Identify main points for each place, e.g. *kind of food, cheap/expensive, suitable for children, easy to get to, open late?*

● **Practice** Talk about and answer the questions in pairs, then as a class.

A

1 The Old Rectory is bound to be much more expensive and up-market.
2 Pasta Piccola
3 Le Cézanne
4 Al's American Diner is near a cinema. You could probably also go to Pasta Piccola and Le Cézanne.
5 Yes, the Old Rectory.

6 Suggestions: boy/girlfriend – Pasta Piccola or Le Cézanne, children – Al's American Diner (children's menus); grandmother – The New Inn or Le Restaurant Parisien; an important business colleague – Le Restaurant Parisien or The Old Rectory.

2 ○ ● **Explanation** This is a freer practice exercise for students, first orally, then in writing. The advertisement (especially the name) usually gives you an idea of what sort of restaurant it is.

● **Practice** Discuss what information the advertisements give. Students work in pairs. They discuss two of the adverts in detail. Then each student writes a description of one of the restaurants as they imagine it to be. This could be done at home.

Options 5

SMALL TALK

Talking about work

○ ● **Explanation** This is a functional exercise. Talking about what you do and asking other people about their work is another common subject of conversation with people you have just met. Students should notice the difference between the job title *I'm a doctor* and the vaguer job description *I'm in computers*.

a/b ● **Practice** Students work in pairs to ask each other about their jobs, as in the examples. Help students with vocabulary and let them use dictionaries to find different ways of describing what they do. Those not in outside employment can talk about what they are studying, or the job they would like to have.

As well as being more specific about a) the employer: *I work for IBM* and b) the job title: *I'm a marketing manager*, students should be able to ask and answer questions providing details, e.g.

A *I am a doctor.*
B *Do you work in a hospital?/Are you a specialist?*
C *Do you work in the Outpatients' Department?*

Students extend the conversation to family and friends' jobs, finding out vocabulary where necessary.

● **Extension**   Students can make a network plan of jobs, showing how they link, e.g. you can be in banking as a computer expert, as a financial adviser, teller, secretary, etc. You can be an accountant working in the hotel trade, furniture manufacturing, the car industry, etc. Make word chains round a central subject, e.g. *banking*. Show the different jobs: *secretary, computer operator, electrician*, etc., and the different departments: *customer services, accounts, loans, personnel*, etc.

More useful vocabulary: *manager, director, representative, assistant, technican, agency*

Students work in pairs, with a different partner if they prefer, to tell each other about their jobs in detail.

ENRICHMENT

The weather

a ○ ● **Explanation**   This section practises words to do with the weather, both the basic ones and other more precise ones.

○ ● **Practice**   Students match weather adjectives to the appropriate pictures they describe.

A					
1 wet	3 sunny	5 foggy
2 windy	4 icy	6 cloudy

b ○ ● **Explanation**   Talking about the weather is as much a social skill as a matter of information. Students should therefore be able to give information about their own country and other countries they know.

○ ● **Warm-up**   Students use their dictionaries to make sure they understand the words listed.

A   Notes on vocabulary:

clear	opposite of cloudy; can be cold or hot weather
mild	not cold; usually used in colder months when weather is warmer than usual
humid	hot, damp weather
chilly	cool weather; more often used of spring/summer/autumn than winter when you expect cold weather
cloudy	skies covered with clouds, not just one or two clouds in the sky.

● **Practice**   Students make true sentences for their country/region's climate by completing the gaps with a form of the verb *be* and an adjective, e.g. *common, rare, usual, normal, frequent*.

c ○ ● **Explanation**   Students listen to sample conversations about the weather and identify the adjectives used to describe each season.

● **Practice**   Play the tape. Students listen and put the adjective in the appropriate column.

A	Winter	Spring	Summer	Autumn
	cold	wet	hot	wet
	clear	chilly	dry	warm
	sunny	windy	humid	foggy
	icy	cloudy		

T.5.4

1 What's the weather like in summer?
  Oh, it's usually hot.
2 Summer? It's usually dry . . . and hot, very hot. It can be very humid in the summer.
3 Is it cold in winter?
  Yes, it's cold. Cold and clear.
  So it can be sunny in winter?
  Yes, that's right.
4 Yes, it isn't wet in winter. It's wet in the spring. The winter is cold, and it's icy at night.
5 When does it rain?
  It's wet here in the spring and autumn.
  It isn't cold in the autumn; its usually warm then.
  It's often foggy in the autumn, though.
6 Is the spring warm?
  No, it's usually chilly. It's windy then, you see. It's a short spring. It's cloudy, wet and chilly, and then, suddenly it's hot and dry, and summer's here.

● **Extension**   Ask students to imagine themselves in various situations where they may talk about the weather, for example: The student is visiting someone in England, who asks about the weather/climate in the student's home region; a foreigner is coming to visit the student, and phones to ask about the weather before coming; two people are talking about a third country, e.g. the USA, which one knows and the other doesn't yet, but is intending to visit soon. For example:

A   *What's the weather like?*
B   *It's very hot at the moment but it can get chilly in the evenings and it sometimes rains at this time of year.*

VOCABULARY

○ ● **Explanation** This vocabulary task focuses on some of the people most involved with health. It asks students to describe their different roles. Students will probably need to use their dictionaries.

● **Practice** Students work in pairs or groups to write definitions using both sets of words. Answers can be compared in class to find the best examples.

A **Possible answers**
A *doctor* tries to *cure* his or her patients.
A *patient* is a person who is *ill*.
*GP*s (general practitioners) are family doctors, who look after people in the *community*, and sometimes visit them *at home*.
A *consultant* is a *senior* hospital doctor.
A *nurse looks after* patients, usually in hospital.
Doctors and nurses are *professionals*.

OUT AND ABOUT

Ordering meals at a restaurant

a/b ○● **Explanation** This exercise practises what to say when ordering a meal in a restaurant.

● **Practice** Students read the words in the box. They then read the sentences below and complete them using one of the words from the box. They listen to check their answers. However, there are various possible answers. Go through the alternatives with the students.

T.5.5

A

Waiter	Are you *ready* to order?
Jane	Yes, we are. Clarissa, what *are you having*?
Clarissa	*I'm having* melon to start with, and then the fish, please.
Roger	And *you*, Paul?
Paul	Soup and the pie *for me*, please.
Roger	Jane?
Jane	Let me think. *I'd like* the soup as well, *followed by* the fish.
Roger	Right. And *I'll have* a mixed salad and then cold beef.
Waiter	*Thank you.*

c ● Make sure students understand the words *host* and *guest*. Then let students work out who are the hosts (Jane and Roger) and who are the guests (Clarissa and Paul).

d ● Students work in groups of five to practise the dialogue. They should practise a few of the roles. Groups can act out their dialogue for the class.

PERSONAL LIFE

○ ● **Explanation** Like the 'Small talk' sections, this exercise practises conversational skills. Students can imagine themselves as famous people asked to take part in a television chat show. This is a fluency rather than an accuracy exercise.

● **Practice** Play the conversation from the Practice section exercise **5a** again, if necessary, to give students a model for an interview, or discuss in class what questions an interviewer can ask to make an interesting conversation on a chat show. Each student should prepare to be both interviewer (prepare questions) and a famous person (have interesting answers and funny anecdotes to tell). Students practise in pairs, then do their interviews in front of the class, either in pairs, or with one interviewer and three different personalities.

The kind of phrases practised here are often used with -*ing* forms, e.g. *Do you like **working** in the film industry/in a hospital?* Remind students that -*ing* noun phrases can be a) used anywhere a noun can be used (i.e. as subject, object, or after prepositions) and b) as long as you like, for example:
I like *reading the papers before breakfast.*
I don't get much time for *reading the papers before breakfast.*
Sitting in the garden with my feet in a bucket of cold water and reading a book is my idea of heaven.

PUZZLE

○ ● **Explanation** This is a comprehension and oral fluency exercise. Students should work out the answers in English. It is not accuracy that is important here, but using the target language to solve a problem.

● **Practice** Students discuss the answers in pairs. They may need to check some food vocabulary in the dictionary.

A A Sam   B Kim   C Jane   D Sue

6
Preview

1 *one/ones*

a ○ ● **Explanation** In English we use *one/ones* as a pronoun to avoid repeating the noun. It is only used for countable nouns: *one* = the singular form and *ones* = the plural form. The four dialogues illustrate the use of *one/ones* and students simply have to match the dialogues to the right pictures.

○ ● **Warm-up** Demonstrate the use of *one/ones* to students in class.
Say: *I need a chair.*
Demonstrate and say: *Here's one. There's another one. Which one shall I have? I'll take this one.*
Then say: *I need more chairs.*
Touch a few and say: *I'll have these ones.*
Ask the students to identify the replacement word for chair(s).
Practise some simple dialogues with the students if you feel it is necessary, e.g.
A   I want a book.
B   Which one do you want?
A   I want the one with the blue cover, etc.

A   I want some pencils.
B   Which ones do you want? etc.

○ ● **Practice** Students read the dialogues and match them to the pictures. Check the answers as a class.

A   A2   B1   C4   D3

Read dialogue 1 again. Ask: What does *one* refer to in **B**'s statement? Students write down the noun phrases before checking the answers as a class.

A
1 one = a soft practice ball
2 ones = trainers
3 one = a tennis racket; ones = metal-framed tennis rackets
4 one = a man/shop assistant

Ask: What kind of word is *one* or *ones*? Students should be able to work out that it is a pronoun since it replaces a noun or noun phrase.

b   ● Students practise the use of *one/ones* by completing the gaps in the dialogues. Let students do the exercise in pairs and then read out one of the dialogues for the class.

A
1 **A** I'd love a cup of tea.
   B I'll bring you *one* now.
2 **A** Why don't you wear red shoes?
   B I want to wear my brown *ones*.
3 **A** Have you got a colour TV?
   B No, I've got a black and white *one*.
4 **A** I really like those flowers.
   B Which *ones*?
   A The pink *ones*.

c   ● Discuss as a class where each of the speakers are and who they might be, e.g. 1 wife/husband at home, 2 parent/child at home, 3 two children at school, 4 two friends out shopping.

2 Relative clauses

a ○ ● **Explanation** Relative clauses give us more information about the person or thing the speaker is talking about. Here students learn the uses of *who, which, that, when, where* as relative pronouns introducing the relative clauses. We use:

who/that for people   *when* for times
which/that for things   *where* for places

○ ● **Warm-up** Read the example. Ask:

Where does Hank live?   London
Where does Archie live?   Longthorpe Castle
Where does Sylvia live?   Lion Place

So Lion Place is the square *where* Sylvia lives.

Do the first sentence with the class. Students are not expected to provide the relative pronouns; here they only have to choose the answers.

○ ● **Practice**   Students work in pairs to underline the answers. They compare their answers with the rest of the class.

A
1 Archie; his father
2 hearts
3 transport minister
4 they keep the crown jewels
5 designer
6 don't have to wait long for
7 a bungalow
8 Londoners
9 American President lives
10 a man first walked on the moon
11 finds very difficult
12 six; sixteenth

b ○ ● **Explanation**   Relative pronouns introduce relative clauses. In **b**, students must identify the relative clauses. Relative clauses give more information on the subject. In the example, we learn more about the place, Lion Place. It is the square *where Sylvia lives*.

○ ● **Practice**   Do the first few sentences with the class. Students find the relative pronouns, and underline the clause that goes with it. Discuss what each clause describes, e.g.

1 *where Archie lives*   describes the place
   which Archie inherited   describes the thing
2 *when you send cards*   describes the time
3 *who interviewed the minister*   describes the person

Then let the students work in pairs to underline the relative clauses. Discuss the rest of the answers in class.

A
4 where they keep the crown jewels (place)
5 who is the designer (person)
6 that you don't have to wait long for (thing)
7 that has no upstairs (thing)
8 that live in London (people)
9 where the American President lives (place)
10 when a man first walked on the moon (time)
11 which he finds very difficult (thing)
12 who had six wives (person)
   when divorce was very unusual (time)

c ○ ● **Presentation**   Which pronouns do we use to introduce relative clauses about a place, time, person, or thing?

○ ● **Practice**   Students have to tick the boxes to show the pronouns that can be used for each. They should work in groups to compare their tables.

A

	who	which	that	where	when
place			(√)	√	
time			(√)		√
people	√		√		
things		√	√		

3 Defining and non-defining relative clauses

a ○ ● **Explanation**   Defining relative clauses are an essential part of a sentence and the sentence often doesn't make sense without it. Non-defining relative clauses, however, give additional information, without which the sentence does still make sense. In writing, it is separated from the main sentences by commas, in speech, by pauses. Students learn to distinguish between the two, first in the written form and then by listening.

T.6.1
A Sylvia is the reporter who interviewed the Minister.
B Henry VIII, who had several wives, was king of England.

○ ● **Practice**   Play the two sentences on the tape. Ask: *Do these two sentences sound the same?* Students will notice that the intonation and punctuation are different. The written form shows that **B** has commas and **A** doesn't. Explain that the clause between commas in **B** is additional information. The sentence: *Henry VIII was king of England* makes sense on its own. The sentence *Sylvia is the reporter* needs more information to be useful.

b ○ ● Students work in pairs to match the sentences to the form of **A** or **B**. They compare their answers as a class.

A   1B 2A 3B 4A 5B 6A 7A 8A 9B

c ○ ● This section explains defining and non-defining clauses to the class.

d ○ ● Read the note in **c** again. We can only replace *who* or *which* with *that* in defining relative clauses.

Students work in groups. They look at exercise **2**
and **3** and identify the relative clauses introduced by
who or *which*. They then work out whether or not
that can be used instead, according to the rules in **c**.

A   **2**   2   It's the castle *that* Archie inherited . . .
   3   Sylvia is the reporter *that* interviewed the
      transport minister.
   5   Poppy, who is a designer, is married to Max.
      (*that* is not possible)
   11   Hank is studying law, which he finds very
      difficult. (*that* is not possible)
   12   King Henry, who had six wives, lived in the
      sixteenth century . . . (*that* is not possible)

   3   1   Tom, who has trained me for years, knows
      me well. (*that* is not possible)
   2   This is the runner *that* holds the 100 metres
      record.
   9   The drug tests, which we all have to take,
      aren't painful. (*that* is not possible)

e ○ ● In their groups, students look for the relative clauses
with *that*. They work out where *that* can be replaced
by *which* and where with *who*.

A   **2**   6   Fast food is food *which* you don't have to wait
      for.
   7   A house *which* has no upstairs floor is called a
      bungalow.
   8   People *who* live in London are called
      Londoners.

   3   7   These are the trainers *which* I wear for
      running.
   8   The tracksuit *which* I bought yesterday is too
      small.

4   Reported speech (1)

○ ● **Presentation**   In this introduction to reported
speech, students see what happens to the present
tense in direct speech when it is changed to reported
speech after *. . . said that . . .* . Reported speech is
continued in Unit 7.

○ ● **Practice**   Read the sentences in direct speech.
Students identify the tenses used. The reported
speech is introduced by *Hank/Max said that . . .* .
Read the statements and ask students to identify the
tenses and say how they have changed. They will
note that the present tenses change to past tenses.

○ ● **Extension**   You may like students to notice that
there are also changes to the pronouns used in the
direct speech. Focus on number 1. Ask: *What else
do you notice changes in reported speech?* Discuss
why *we* in direct speech changes to *they* in reported
speech.

5   Vocabulary

○ ● **Explanation**   This is dictionary work. Students can
categorize vocabulary into two groups: sport and
medicines/illness.

○ ● **Warm-up**   Read the list of words and give students
an opportunity to practise their pronunciation.
Students may use their dictionary for words they are
not sure of.

○ ● **Practice**   Students work in pairs to list the words
under the correct heading. They can check their lists
with the rest of the class.

A

Sport		Medicine/illness
race	team	aspirin
run	trials	dose
spirit	athlete	cold cure
win	athletics	hypochondriac
banned substances		powders
distance		

6   *used to (be)*

○ ● **Explanation**   Students practise *used to* to describe
past states and situations that are no longer true.
They compare how Joshua Jones used to be with
what he is like now.

● **Warm-up**   Students study the two pictures of
Joshua Jones when he was a classical musician and
as he is now – a pop star. They find as many
differences as possible between them.

○ ● **Practice**   Students study the example sentences and
then write more sentences on the same model. Ask
them to compare this structure with their own
language. Check answers with the class.

A   **Sample answers**
He used to wear glasses, but now he doesn't.
He used to play a classical guitar, but now he plays
an electric guitar.
He used to wear formal clothes, but now he wears
informal clothes.

Olympic hurdle

T.6.2 Hank and Tom come to Max's office, looking for Rita. She has gone to Manchester, where the Olympic trials are being held. Max thinks she has gone to watch, but Tom and Hank know she is taking part. Sylvia arrives bringing bad news: Rita won her race, but the drug test was positive. Max is surprised, because he knows how careful Rita is about drugs and in fact any form of stimulant, even coffee. Reporters are outside Rita's flat and Max's office; Rita arrives and sneaks in the back way. She tells the others what has happened, but says she has never taken drugs. The drug found is Cladoxin. Max remembers the name, and looks for his cold cure powders. He remembers that he put one in a glass of juice for himself the day before, and realizes that Rita must have drunk it by mistake. Max gets in touch with his lawyer, determined to help Rita clear her name.

The people in this episode

Max is busy as usual, and is only mildly interested to learn that Rita is an Olympic-class athlete. However, when he hears what has happened, he shows that he does know his staff well, and has no doubts about her innocence. He also shows how quick-thinking he is. He at once makes the connection between his cold cure and the drug in Rita's test. He wastes no time in contacting his lawyer and intends to help her sort out the problem.

Hank is more relaxed with Max than before, and teases him a little. His father, as usual, overshadows him when there is something to be done.

Tom is obviously now on good terms with everyone. He is knowledgeable about athletics, and reserves judgement on Rita's test result. However, he is quick to see what Max is getting at when he produces his cold cure.

Sylvia is sympathetic towards Rita, but still excited by the story, and keen to get at the facts.

Rita is understandably bewildered, and horrified at the thought of being banned from athletics. She feels at ease enough with Max and the others to come to the office when she is in trouble, and to tell them what happened.

● **Warm-up** Look at the picture, and identify all the people in it. Ask:

Is Rita OK?
Why do you think Max is holding a packet up?
What do you think has happened/is happening?

Play the cassette. Ask the students:

What is the main subject of the episode?
Do you now know why Max is holding the packet up?

Play the cassette again, section by section. Ask the students what has happened in each section. Ask questions like these:

Why is Rita in Manchester?
Why does Tom know about athletics?
What news does Sylvia bring?
What did Rita's drug test show?
How did Rita take the drug?
What is Max's reaction?

Performance 6

COMPREHENSION

1 ○ ● **Explanation** These are quick-check questions on understanding the story. The correct statements are 3, 10, 12, 16.

○ ● **Practice** Read the statements together and decide which ones are correct. Then students work in pairs to correct the others either orally or in writing. They check their answers with the rest of the class.

A
1 No, he wants to go to the cinema.
2 No, she's at the Olympic trials in Manchester.
4 No, his mother was in the Australian team.
5 No, it's cold and wet in England.
6 No, she won her race.
7 No, she says Rita is in big trouble.
8 No, she isn't at home, she's at the office.
9 No, she never takes an aspirin.
11 No, John Dugdale is the head coach.
13 No, he telephones his lawyer.
14 Yes, he does – he's a hypochondriac.
15 Yes, he does. He takes them all the time.
17 No, he's Max's lawyer.

2 ○ ● **Explanation** Students use the context of the story to work out the meaning of these idiomatic phrases. They can explain in other English words, or (if the class have the same mother tongue) translate, if necessary.

● **Practice**   Students work in pairs, then compare answers with another pair, before checking the answers as a class. If they cannot work out one or two, then they can use a dictionary.

A   **Suggested explanations**

won three Oscars = won three prizes at the USA film awards ceremony

trying for an Olympic place = trying to win a place on the national Olympics team

takes an interest in = is interested in (in a paternal way)

the test was positive = the test found traces of a banned drug

they've suspended me = she has been dropped from the team until the drug problem is explained

they'll ban me for life = will stop her taking part in athletics for the rest of her life

that rings a bell = I remember something in connection with that

do not exceed the stated dose = do not take more of this medicine than it recommends on the bottle

hypochondriac = a person who thinks he or she is ill all the time

PRACTICE

1 ○ ● **Explanation**   Students practise recognizing relative clauses and identifying the type. It is important to be able to distinguish the two types for clear communication: intonation of the two types is quite different, and using the wrong intonation makes it more difficult for a listener to understand the meaning. This is why the comma is also important – it shows where the voice changes.

○ ● **Practice**   Students work in pairs. They read through the episode, underlining or copying down the relative clauses. Then they decide whether they are defining (D) or non-defining (ND) clauses. Students underline the relative pronouns and relative adverbs (*where* and *when*). They compare their answers with the class.

A   It's that French film *which* won three Oscars. **D**
Rita's the one *who* runs. **D**
Manchester is the place *where* the Olympic trials are. **D**
. . . her flat, *which* is surrounded by reporters. **ND**
. . . my trainer, *who* knows I don't take drugs, came and told me. **ND**
John Dugdale, *who* is the head coach, was furious. **ND**

2 ○ ● **Explanation**   Students practise using the correct relative pronoun. Remind students of the differences. See exercise **2** of the Preview and the Grammar Summary on page 75.

○ ● **Practice**   Students work in pairs to fill in the gaps. Let the students read out their answers to the class and check their intonation.

A   Yesterday, sports enthusiasts *who* were in Deansgate Stadium in Manchester, *where* the Olympic Trials took place, enjoyed a thrilling day. The trials, *which* were a great success, delighted the England captain, Harold Barclay. 'I'm looking forward to the day *when* this team wins Olympic gold,' says Barclay. 'The team *which/that* we have chosen is terrific. Some of the younger athletes *who/that* took part are world-beaters.'

Dent and Alston, *who* both won medals at the last Olympics, are running again. In the first heat, *which* Dent won, a young girl, *who* has never taken part in the trials before, came second. 'She's good enough to win a medal,' says a trainer *who/that* watched her. 'Esther's good for a gold medal, I'm sure,' says another athlete *who/that** we spoke to.

*__Note__   The older form *whom* when the pronoun is the object is still seen today, especially in written texts. However, *who/that* is much more common today.

3 ○ ● **Explanation**   Here is written practice in punctuating relative clauses (using commas to mark off non-defining clauses).

○ ● **Practice**   Remind students that commas separate the non-defining relative clause from the main sentence. As a class, read the sentences. Work out which are defining and which are non-defining clauses. Let the students work in pairs to try to find the answers but then discuss them as a class in order to clear up any confusion. Remind students that relative clauses are an essential part of the sentence, without which the sentence usually does not make sense. Non-defining clauses simply add information to a sentence but the sentence does make sense without it.

A   1 No commas
2 Max, who lives opposite, is a rich man.
3 This cold cure, which doesn't work, is called Cladoxin.

4 No commas
5 Last year, when I was 21, I went to America.
6 No commas
7 Lion Place, where Toby lives, is very pretty.
8 No commas

4 a ○ ● **Explanation** This exercise gives students written practice in relative clauses. Students have to choose the appropriate relative pronouns and then complete a sentence.

Note Time and place relative clauses such as *the time when . . .* (=the time at which) and *the place where . . .* (=the place at which) should be treated with care. In these sentences, the noun preceding the clause will always be a time-word, e.g. *time, afternoon, year, day*, etc., or a place-word or place-name, e.g. *garden, place, roof, town, Manchester*, etc.

○ ● **Practice** Students can work alone or in pairs to complete the sentences.

A **Possible answers**
The Antarctic is a place *where there is always snow.*
My neighbour is a person *who/that likes gardening.*
Lions are animals *which/that live in Africa.*
London is a place *where a lot of tourists go.*

b ○ ● Students work in pairs to produce sentences with a relative clause to describe the characters and places in *Streets Ahead*.

A **Possible answers**
Toby is an architect who used to *work for Max.*
Longthorpe Castle is the castle *where Archie lives/which Archie owns/that Archie inherited.*
Archie is the man *who/that used to be a racing driver/that lives in a castle.*
Sylvia is the reporter *who/that works for Network TV.*
Lion Place is the square *where the main characters live.*

5 a ○ ● **Explanation** This is a listening task to practise *used to.*

○ ● **Practice** Play the cassette through once. Study the picture and talk about how the room has changed. Play the cassette again. Students make notes about particular parts of the room, noting down how it used to look. They list those things that are still in the room: the fireplace, the chair, the table, and the shelves.

b ● This is an opportunity for a discussion, either in pairs or as a class.

T.6.3 This room used to be much darker. The walls used to have a greeny-brown paper on them. It was always untidy. It used to be the family room. We used to do our homework on the table, and Dad used to read the paper in here, and listen to the radio. His chair used to be over there, near the fire. There were heavy velvet curtains, I think, and small rugs on the floor. My brothers and I used to play trains with them. Mum used to get furious. There was just one central light. It was quite a dark room – dark wallpaper, dark curtains, brown furniture, not much light. I used to have a box under the table with my toys in it, when I was little. My brothers used to keep things on those shelves. They used to be brown, then. It's all very different now.

A **Possible answers**
This text describes a typical 1950s room. The person speaking is looking back on her childhood. She is different because she is older, but also, styles of living have changed considerably – for example, lighting, colours, TV, music centre, central heating, fitted carpets. She has a very comfortable life.

● **Extension** Students can imagine a room or building they know which is much older than they are, and write a similar text about the people who used to live there or who used the building. The emphasis would be on imaginative details. If the school building is old, groups can use this as a basis. The students could read out the most imaginative descriptions.

6 ○ ● **Explanation** In this exercise, students practise *used to* while exchanging personal information about how they used to look, what they used to do, believe in, etc. The students could bring in an old photograph of themselves. This should be regarded as a fluency exercise, although the students can write a paragraph for homework.

● **Practice** Each student prepares a few notes to use in a discussion. Students then talk in groups, e.g.
A *I used to wear jeans all the time.*
B *So did I and I never wore skirts.*
C *I used to wear long skirts and do yoga!*

Note Although *used to* is often taught with a restricted meaning: *I used to do this = but I no longer do*, it is also used when referring to the past, with no indication that things have changed. For example, remembering the town where you lived as a child, you might say, *There used to be a wonderful baker's on the corner*. This doesn't mean the baker's is no longer there. You just do not have information about the present situation, only about how things were in the past.

7 ○ ● **Explanation**   This exercise gives students oral practice of pronouns *one/ones* and revision of comparatives.

○ ● **Warm-up**   To generate vocabulary, play a memory game. Give students a minute to study the picture. Then ask students to close their books and give them a few minutes to write down as much as they can remember about the sports clothes: what they were and what they looked like.

● **Practice**   Students work in pairs to discuss the clothes in the picture as in the example. They must explain why they (do not) like a particular piece of clothing talking about its style, price, colour, etc. They can then compare their preferences.

8 ○ ● **Explanation**   This is a practice exercise for students first learning about reported speech. Students have to write exactly what each person said, taking care to use the right tense and pronoun.

○ ● **Practice**   Students work in pairs to do the exercise. They check their answers in class.

A
1 Your drug test is positive.
2 I never take drugs.
3 Rita isn't in her flat.
4 I'm going to talk to my lawyer.
5 Everything's going to be fine.
6 I hope so.

PRONUNCIATION

1 ○ ● **Explanation**   More practice in word stress.

○ ● **Practice**   Say the words aloud together. Then let students underline the stress. Alternatively, let students say the words and decide the stress in pairs, and then check their pronunciation as a class.

A

Olympics	preservatives	petrol	athlete
Manchester	teleprinter	stadium	blood test
positive	hypochondriac	exceed	substance

2 ○ ● **Explanation**   This listening exercise gives students practice in recognizing the main sentence stress. The different stress gives implicit meaning to the sentence.

● **Practice**   Play the cassette and let students listen to the pairs of sentences. They note the sentences where the stress changes. The stress differs in a, c, e, and h.

● **Extension**   After completing the exercise, you can ask students to work out two short dialogues, each containing the two sentences from either a, c, e or h, to illustrate the different pronunciations. Students act out their dialogues making sure they get the sentence stress right to convey their meaning.

T.6.4
A
a Rita **likes** French films/Rita likes **French** films. (**D**)
b Do you know about **athletics**, Tom?/Do you know about **athletics**, Tom? (**S**)
c I used to watch a **lot** of races/I used to watch a lot of **races**. (**D**)
d I've got **work** to do/I've got **work** to do. (**S**)
e She's in **big** trouble/She's in big **trouble**. (**D**)
f What's all **this**?/What's all **this**? (**S**)
g Did you have a glass of **orange** juice?/Did you have a glass of **orange** juice? (**S**)
h I put two **powders** in my glass/I put **two** powders in my glass. (**D**)

3 ○ ● **Explanation**   Students practise matching words with different spelling and the same pronunciation.

● **Practice**   Read out the list of words once. Students then work in pairs to find the rhyming pairs. They discuss their answers in class.

A

fast/passed	boot/suit	bed/said	spend/friend
hour/shower	got/what	heat/feet	
in it/minute	wait/gate	clear/here	

READING

○ ● **Explanation**   The reading exercise gives students an opportunity to compare and contrast two people's strong opinions on a subject: to identify their differences and where they agree.

○ ● **Warm-up**   Before starting on the passage, let students study the list of words in exercise **1** and try to guess the meanings.

- **Practice**   Students read the passage through quickly once.

   Have you heard of Daley Thompson?
   What kind of person do you think he is?
   What do you think of the doctor?

1 ○ - **Explanation**   Students work out the meaning of the words and phrases in the context of the passage and translate them into their own language. They can use their dictionaries.

- **Practice**   Students identify the sentences where the words and phrases occur. They discuss them in class and translate them. Did they guess the right meaning before they read the passage?

2 ○ - **Explanation**   This is a general comprehension exercise and requires students to study the opinions of the two people and sort out their differences.

- **Practice**   Students work in small groups to discuss their answers. They should remember that they are comparing the opinions of a top professional athlete and of a doctor who speaks from an objective viewpoint.

A   Daley Thompson and the doctor do not agree with each other about drugs. Neither of them believe in drugs, but they have different opinions about them. Daley Thompson does not approve of anyone taking drugs. The doctor says it is up to the athletes to decide for themselves, as long as they understand the risks. They both understand why athletes take drugs – they want to win. The doctor is rather scornful and says that athletes will do almost anything to win, and do not care about the future. Daley Thompson feels sorry for those athletes who feel they need something to help them work hard enough to do well. But he is angry about the effect taking drugs has had on sport and young people. He feels strongly that they should not be allowed. The doctor thinks that this would be difficult to put into practice, as you cannot test for some of them yet.

3 ○ - This is a writing exercise using the information in the text. Students could mention these points:

   Athletes take drugs because they think it is the only way for them to improve; it allows them to work hard at their training; it can help them win a gold medal; other athletes are taking them.

- **Extension**   Students discuss their own opinions of the use of drugs in sport.

You may like to ask students to prepare for the discussion. They can find articles on the subject in their local magazines. For example, there have been articles on the use of drugs among cyclists which have caused several deaths. Ask:

Why do you think sports people take drugs?
(Talk about: the pressure to qualify for a team because of the access to top training, access to competition, travel, money, sponsorship. Then the pressure to maintain top performance; for professional sports people it is their income, etc.)

Do athletes know enough about the long-term effects of taking drugs?
Is there enough information about the effect drugs have on sports people in different sports?
Who should decide whether or not drugs should be allowed to be used by sports people?
What is the hypocrisy that the doctor refers to?
(You may also want to discuss the fact that drugs have become big business. The doctor refers to new drugs becoming available for which there is no test and which are not yet banned. There are also methods of improving the quality of the blood by blood transfusion, to improve performance. These methods are also dangerous but not yet illegal or detectable.)

Options 6

GRAMMAR

○ - **Explanation**   This exercise is intended to help students use English flexibly. Reducing relative clauses to a phrase using *with* is very common in everyday English when the relative clause contains *has (got)/have (got)*.

- **Practice**   Students convert the sentences, either orally in class, or writing in pairs.

A
1 She's the tall blond woman with glasses.
2 Eleanor's the dark woman with two dogs.
3 My car is the one with a sun-roof.
4 Give it to Ben – he's the boy with the freckles.
5 Mountain bikes are the ones with thick tyres.

FURTHER PRACTICE

o ● **Explanation** This is further practice in the present perfect to distinguish between *been* and *gone*, where students often make mistakes.

o ● **Warm-up** Look at the two illustrations and read the examples. Do students understand the difference? Is there a difference in their language? Since *has gone* implies 'has not returned', ask students to think of a situation where someone could say *I've gone . . .*, e.g. on a note left for someone before leaving: *John. I've gone to the shops. Back soon.*

o ● **Practice** Students work in small groups or as a class to complete the sentences, then translate them. They may find that their language does not distinguish here.

A
1 I've *been* to Madrid twice.
2 I've *been* in an aeroplane.
3 Where's Janet? She's *gone* shopping.
4 I haven't *been* to Seville this year, but I went last year.
5 Max has *gone* to New York. He'll be back in two weeks.

SMALL TALK

a o ● **Explanation** Successful small talk is mostly a question of recognizing the situation and then using the right phrase.

● **Practice** As a class, match the questions and answers. Then let students practise the dialogues in pairs.

o ● **Extension** In small groups, students think of a slightly different situation for each, and discuss whether the same question and response still applies, e.g. in 2d would it be correct if the woman was still reading the paper? In 4c would it be all right if someone else in the room was obviously cold, or the weather was very bad outside? Would it be all right if you were visiting someone in their home and found the room very hot? Students can act out the new situations in pairs, and let the rest of the class say whether this is the best thing to say in the new situation.

A 1b; C   2d; B   3a; A   4c; D

b ● Students work in small groups to discuss other situations where the original dialogues in **a** would be correct, e.g. in a bus/plane; on a park bench; at a theatre; in a sports stadium/restaurant/cinema.

TIME

a o ● **Explanation** This section practises words and phrases to describe time. In **a**, students practise two ways of saying clock time. Exercise **b** picks up many of the common mistakes in the use of verbs with time expressions. How common they are depends on usage in the mother tongue. Students identify the errors and correct them. Exercise **c** practises time expressions by asking students to put them in the right chronological order.

● **Practice** Students work in pairs or alone to write (and say) the two ways of telling the time. Check as a class.

A
1 (a) quarter to six/five forty-five
2 (a) quarter past four/four-fifteen
3 half past one/one-thirty

b o ● Students work in small groups or as a class to identify the errors. They must write them correctly. Students read out the corrected sentences and the class says whether they agree with the correction or not.

A
1 They're coming at twenty *to* one.
2 *I've* lived here since 1989.
3 We were here *yesterday* or we *will be* here tomorrow.
4 Europe *will be* warmer in twenty years' time.
5 She's live*d* here *for* three years.
6 I'll be there at five *past* ten. (However, *after* is American usage.)

c ● These simply need practice. Put a large calendar on the board. Identify 'today' and then point to different days. Encourage students to think of the correct time expression as quickly as possible. Then let students work out the correct chronological order alone. Compare answers as a class.

A
1 the week before last	6 today
2 last week	7 tomorrow
3 five days ago	8 the day after
4 the day before yesterday	tomorrow
5 yesterday	9 in three days

7
Preview

1 Reported speech (2)

a Statements

○ ● **Presentation**   In Unit 6, students were introduced to reported speech. They should not find it too difficult to progress from their knowledge that the present tense in direct speech changes to the past in indirect or reported speech.

○ ● **Warm-up**   Look at the pictures of Sylvia, Anna, and Suzi. The speech bubbles show the exact words of the speaker. In the first drawing, Sylvia talks to Anna. In the second picture, Anna tells Suzi what Sylvia said. Ask students: *What is the difference between the two statements?*

○ ● **Practice**   Work as a class. Read what else Sylvia says. Compare Sylvia's and Anna's statements. Say: *Let's look at the verbs first. What tense does Sylvia use? What tense does Anna use?* Complete the chart together.

A	Direct speech	Reported speech
	am/is	was
	have/has	had
	will	would
	can	could
	present simple	past simple
	past simple	past perfect
	present perfect	past perfect

The rule is that in reported speech (when the reporting verb is in the past tense), the tenses move one tense further back into the past.

b Questions

○ ● **Presentation**   There are two main ways of forming questions in English:
1 with a question word: *Where are they?*
2 by inverting the subject and verb with the auxiliary or *do/does*: *Are you free? Does she know him?*

These affect the way we report a question.

○ ● **Warm-up**   Look at the pictures of Sylvia, Anna, and Suzi. Read Sylvia's questions. Compare the way Anna reports Sylvia's questions to Suzi. Ask: *What is different?* Students will be able to identify that the tenses change as for statements; they may notice that the word order is different and they will probably notice the use of *if* and *when*.

○ ● **Practice**   Students discuss the answers in pairs before discussing it as a class.

A	
	1 The word order changes back to normal sentence order: subject then verb.
	2 The auxiliaries *do/does* disappear as they are not needed in normal sentence order.
	3 *If* (or *whether*) is used when there is no question (*wh-*) word and the direct question begins with an auxiliary: *do, are, can*, etc.

2 Vocabulary

○ ● **Explanation**   Students identify the words and phrases concerned with the theatre and drama.

○ ● **Warm-up**   Read the list and give students the chance to practise their pronunciation. They may use a dictionary to help them for this exercise.

Practice   Students work in pairs to list the words to do with drama and the theatre. They compare their list with the rest of the class. Make sure they know the meanings of the other words, too.

A		
studio	drama	theatre
rehearsal	actor	a part
audition (n)	audition (v)	director

3   Past participles

Explanation   Students confuse some past participles and past tense forms. This gives them an opportunity to identify some of these difficulties and learn the correct forms. Encourage students to use their dictionaries to help them.

Practice   Students work in pairs to sort the list of words into the right columns and to complete the columns with the missing forms. Check the answers as a class, practising the pronunciation at the same time.

A	Verb	Past simple	Past participle
	go	went	*gone*
	be	*was/were*	been
	take	*took*	taken
	see	saw	*seen*
	do	*did*	done
	come	*came*	come
	tell	told	told
	stand	stood	stood
	hear	heard	heard
	think	thought	thought
	have	had	had
	say	said	said
	spend	spent	spent
	read	read	read
	let	let	let
	drive	*drove*	driven
	meet	met	met
	make	made	made
	mean	meant	meant
	get	got	got
	hold	held	held
	sell	sold	sold
	begin	began	*begun*
	sit	sat	sat
	win	won	won

4   *when* clauses (time-free)

a   **Presentation**   Students learnt the first conditional: *if*+present tense+*will*, and the time-free or zero conditional: *if*+present tense+present tense in Unit 5. This is another form of the time-free conditional. We use it to describe habitual situations or general truths.

Practice   Play the cassette through once. Stop after each interview. Students write down what each person's ambition is. Play the cassette again without stopping for students to check their answers.

T.7.1		
	Sylvia	Right, now, can I ask you all about your hopes for the future? What do you want to do, Michael?
	Michael	I'd like to work in a bank.
	Sylvia	Do you think you can get a job in a bank?
	Michael	Don't know. When my father brings home his newspaper, I always read the money pages. I know a bit about banking.
	Sylvia	What about you, Donna?
	Donna	I'm hoping to get into teaching.
	Sylvia	Have you done any teaching?
	Donna	Well, my aunt's a teacher in a village school, and when I stay with her, I help in the classroom with the little ones.
	Sylvia	Claire, what's the future got for you?
	Claire	I'm hoping to go to the polytechnic.
	Sylvia	What do you want to study?
	Claire	I hope I can do electronics. When I have time, I often go to the big computer shows.
	Sylvia	David?
	David	I want to travel.
	Sylvia	Have you travelled?
	David	Not much. When I can, I do, though. France, Spain. Places like that.

A	
	Michael would like to work in a bank.
	Donna is hoping to get into teaching.
	Claire is hoping to go to the polytechnic to do electronics.
	David wants to travel.

b   What can students remember about the interviews? Students discuss what each of the school leavers has done so far towards achieving their ambition.

A Michael reads the money pages.
Donna helps her aunt in the village school when she goes to visit her.
Claire goes to the big computer shows.
David travels when he can. He has been to Spain and France.

c ○ ● Students try to remember the time-free clauses beginning with *when* and write them down. Play the cassette. Stop after each interview to give students the opportunity to check their sentences. Students then work in pairs to identify the tense used in the clauses. As a class, discuss why the present tense is used. Ask: *Is the present tense also used in the main clauses?* Remind students that time-free clauses do not depend on any particular time or situation. (See the Grammar Summary on page 63.)

All the world's a stage

T.7.2 Suzi is auditioning for a part with the National Youth Theatre. She meets a young man called Alistair at the door. He has also come to audition. A member of staff directs them to Room 3 where they have to register. Suzi is not needed yet, and as she is waiting, Sylvia appears. She is working on a TV programme on drama. Suzi explains that she has come back from Spain for the audition, and is hoping to get into films. Sylvia is sceptical, but Suzi is unconcerned, and question Sylvia about the standard of the auditions. Her turn comes, and Sylvia goes to watch.
After her piece, Suzi is a bit disappointed. She does not think she has done well. She and Sylvia have a cup of coffee. Suzi gossips about Archie and Anna, and interrogates Sylvia about her relationship with Toby. Sylvia is glad not to have to answer her as Suzi is called to read for a part.

The people in this episode

Suzi is her usual confident self, starting a conversation with Alistair and greeting Sylvia in a very relaxed way. She is less confident after the audition, thinking she has done badly because they only heard one of her pieces. She is obviously serious about acting. Although older, Suzi has not lost the habit of asking embarrassing questions.

Sylvia is seen as friendly and at ease with her work. She takes an interest in Suzi, but does not want to gossip about Archie and Anna or talk about Toby.

● **Warm-up** Look at the picture. Ask:
Who do you recognize?
Why do you think they are there?
Why are the other people there?
What is Suzi doing?
Play the cassette of the whole episode.

Now play the cassette section by section. Ask questions about each section.
Who is talking?
What are they talking about?
Do you learn anything new about the main characters' lives?

Ask questions like these:
Why are Suzi and Alistair there?
Why is Sylvia there?
What is Suzi doing for her audition?
How does Suzi feel about her audition?
What does Suzi talk about with Sylvia?
What brings their conversation to an end?

Performance 7

COMPREHENSION

1 ○ ● **Explanation** These questions test general understanding of the text.

○ ● **Practice** Read the questions as a class. Students can read the text once more. Then they work in groups to discuss their answers without referring to the text.

A 1 At the auditions/At reception
2 In Room 3
3 Alistair
4 In Room 3/In the cafeteria
5 In Room 5
6 Shakespeare
7 She's hoping to get into films.
8 In London at the TV studios

2 ○ ● **Explanation**   Students complete a passage which is a summary of the text. It tests not only comprehension of the story, but also revises grammar items.

○ ● **Practice**   Students work in pairs to complete the text without referring to the story. They compare their answers with the rest of the class, and then look back at the story to check any remaining doubts.

A   Suzi arrived at the theatre and met a young man called Alistair Bond, who was also there for the NYT *auditions*. Alistair wondered which *room* the auditions were in. Someone *who* worked at the theatre told *them* to go to Room 3. They went down the stairs and someone asked to see their *cards*. Suzi had to *wait*, but Alistair went to Room 5 at once. Then Suzi *met* Sylvia and asked her what she was *doing* there. Sylvia *said* she was doing a special *programme* about drama. Suzi said she had *come* back from Spain for the audition. Sylvia said she was going to *watch* the auditions and *asked* Suzi what she was doing for her audition. Then someone called Suzi's name and *told* her to go to Room 4. The director *wanted* to hear Suzi's Shakespeare piece but he *didn't* want to hear her other piece. Suzi left, feeling depressed. Sylvia said she thought Suzi's audition *was* good. Then they *went* for a coffee and talked. Suzi *asked* a lot of questions, but Sylvia didn't *answer* them. She said it *was* none of Suzi's business. Then they *called* Suzi's name again, and told *her* to go to the main hall. The *director* wanted her to read for a part.

PRACTICE

1 ○ ● **Explanation**   Students identify indirect/reported questions and work out the direct questions in them.

Note   Indirect questions (or reported questions) can be introduced by verbs other than *ask*, such as *wonder, want to know, demand*. Note also the special type of indirect question with *tell*, which means 'Here is the answer to this question.'.

○ ● **Practice**   Students work in pairs. They work through Episode 7 and identify all the indirect questions. Write them on the board. Then as a class work out what the direct questions are, and write them underneath.

A   Do you know who's taking the auditions?
    Who's taking the auditions?
I don't know if the director is taking them.
    Is the director taking them?
We'll tell you which room to go to.
    Which room shall I go to?
I don't know if you're on the list.
    Are you on the list?
I asked the director if I could watch.*
    Can I watch?
(Please) don't tell me what I did wrong.
    What did I do wrong?
I wonder if Archie is in love with her.
    Is Archie in love with her?
I don't know if Archie's in love with Anna.
    Is Archie in love with Anna?

*****Note**   An example of a reported question. The others are all indirect questions, i.e. with no reporting verb.

2a○ ● **Explanation**   This provides practice in indirect questions. See the notes for exercise **1**.

○ ● **Practice**   Students work in pairs to identify the speakers. They need this information for **b**. They will probably need to refer back to the story to do this exercise.

A | | |
|---|---|
| 2 Suzi to Sylvia | 7 Suzi to the director |
| 3 Sylvia to Suzi | 8 Suzi to Sylvia |
| 4 Suzi to Sylvia | 9 Suzi to Sylvia |
| 5 Suzi to Sylvia | 10 Staff member to Suzi |
| 6 Sylvia to Suzi | |

b ○ ● Students practise reporting questions. Remind students of the things they have to consider: *if/whether* or *wh-*, tenses, word order, pronouns. Students have not yet come across the change of *here* in direct speech, to *there* in indirect speech. Use number 2 as an example and write it on the board. Students work in pairs to write the answers.

A **Sample answers**
2 Suzi asked Sylvia what she was doing there.
3 Sylvia asked Suzi how she was.
4 Suzi wanted to know if Sylvia had seen any of the auditions/asked Sylvia if she had seen any of the auditions.
5 Suzi asked Sylvia if/wondered if the others were good.
6 Sylvia wanted to know/didn't know what Suzi was doing for her audition.
7 Suzi asked the director if he wanted to hear her other piece.
8 Suzi wanted to know if Sylvia was in London all the time/Suzi asked Sylvia if she was in London all the time.
9 Suzi wondered if/wanted to know if Anna was there when Sylvia went (to Longthorpe).
10 A member of staff asked if Suzi was in there.

3 ○ ● **Explanation** Students practise reporting a conversation. It is not important that the conversation is correct, but that they are practising reported speech.

● **Practice** Students work as a class. They try to remember what Suzi and Sylvia said about Archie. Put their version on the board and then they compare their answers with the story.

A **Possible answer**
Suzi said that she thought Anna was keen on Archie, and wondered if Archie was in love with Anna. Sylvia replied that she didn't know if Archie was in love with Anna, and she didn't think it was any of Suzi's business.

○ ● **Extension** It is also useful to be able to report what people said from the mother tongue into English. If possible, bring in a short conversation from the radio or television containing a lot of questions. Ask the students to imagine they are explaining it to a foreign visitor. Don't insist on grammatical correctness.

4a ○ ● **Explanation** In this listening task, students have to work out the original conversation from Alistair's report and act it out as a dialogue.

○ ● **Practice** Students look at what the director says. Play the cassette once through for students to listen to the conversation between Alistair and Suzi. Then students work in pairs to work out exactly what the producer said. Play the cassette again, pausing after Alistair's answers to give students enough time to work it out and write it down. Play the tape a third time for the students to check their answers.

A **Producer**
Yes, so did I.
No, I don't think so.
Yes, she forgot some words, probably because she was nervous.
It's a very low voice for the part.

T.7.3 **AB** . . . There were two of them there, the director and the producer. I was just outside the door. I had to speak to the producer, you see.
Suzi What did they say about me?
AB Er . . . They both said they liked your Shakespeare piece. But the producer also said she didn't want to hear your other piece.
Suzi Did they say anything about the Shakespeare piece?
AB The director said you were a bit nervous, but that was normal. The producer said you forgot some words, but that was probably because you were nervous.
Suzi What about my voice? Did he like it?
AB I don't know if he liked it. He said it was a bit like Amanda's voice. I think Amanda's his wife. The producer said it was a very low voice for the part.
Suzi Did she say that?
AB Well, yes.
Suzi I haven't got the part, then.
AB No, not at all. The director said you looked right for the part, and your Shakespeare piece was good. In fact, he said it was very good. The producer said that you weren't bad and that they should put your name on their list.
Suzi Oh well, I won't go home yet, then.

b • Students act out the conversation, using the script from **a**. Having heard Alistair's report, they may like to add additional words or sentences. Students work in pairs to practise the dialogue and then a few pairs act it out for the class.

5 a ○ • **Explanation** This exercise is to practise putting reported speech into direct speech and vice versa. To make it more interesting, it is the beginning of a story. Once the students have finished the exercises they will have formed ideas about what is happening and can finish the story.
First we are introduced to the characters. We know Jack needs money and has asked his sister to ask his uncle. Our sympathies are with Jack and Mary when we look at the three questions, even before we read their conversation.

○ • **Practice** Read the questions and ask students to think about them as they read the dialogue. Once the students have read it, discuss the answers to the questions, then let two students act the dialogue for the class.

A 1 Mary is angry with her uncle because he won't give Jack the money he needs.
2 Uncle Fred is calm.
3 Mary agrees to stay.

In pairs, students read the dialogue again, and identify the different kinds of statement. Discuss the answers in class.

A **A positive statement** I've said what I wanted to say.
A negative statement You won't give Jack his money.
A question Why?/Can I make a suggestion?
A request Please come and sit down for a moment.
An order Put it in front of the garage next door, then come back.
A promise I'll come back.
An explanation My neighbour's away./I'm in a hurry.
An agreement Oh, all right./Yes, you have.
A comment That's a nice car you've got.

---

b • Read the next part of the story. The emphasis shifts away from poor Jack now as the story unfolds. We begin to get more information and our sympathies are moving to Uncle Fred. By the end of this passage, we understand completely why Uncle Fred has not given Jack any money and we are beginning to get

impatient with Mary who insists on defending her brother, even when he is clearly doing something wrong. In fact, Mary is being used by her brother. Ask check questions:

What do you think of Uncle Fred/Mary/Jack now?
What does Mary think of her uncle?
What is Jack's problem?
Do you think he's changed?

c ○ • Students work out the original conversation between Jack and Uncle Fred from Uncle Fred's reported conversation with Mary. Remind them to take care with tenses, word order, pronouns. They can work in pairs. Ask a pair to read out the dialogue for the class to check answers.

A **Jack** I promise *to stay* away *from the races* in *future.* I *find the races* boring.
UF Yes, they *are.* What are you *doing these* days?
Jack I'*m spending* my time at *home* reading.
UF Do *you read racing* books?
Jack No, I *don't.* I *read good* books. I *like* novels. Uncle Fred, *could* you *give* me some money? I *need* it *to buy* furniture. It'*s* my *money* anyway.
UF Stay *away from the races*, then I'*ll give* you your *money!*

---

6 ○ • **Explanation** In the last part of this story, Mary's loyalty to her brother doesn't shift but we are clearly on Uncle Fred's side and we know he will find out the truth and will help Jack.

a • **Practice** Read the passage with the students. Let students practise the dialogue in pairs, then ask a pair to read it out for the class. Ask check questions:

How does Uncle Fred feel?
How does Mary feel?
Who do you have more faith/confidence in?
What do you think of Mary/Uncle Fred now?

b ○ • Students work in pairs to report Mary and Uncle Fred's conversation. They compare their answers as a class.

A **Possible answer**
Mary said she didn't believe it because Jack never told lies. Uncle Fred told her it was true. Jack had been speaking to some men who had looked a bit dangerous. He said Jack had given them the money. Mary said that Jack was in trouble. Uncle Fred asked her why she thought that. She said she knew

---

him because he was her brother. She said that they had to help him. Uncle Fred told her to calm herself. He said they would follow him to the races that weekend. He told Mary not to worry. They would find out what was going on.

In pairs, students finish the story. This can be done in a number of ways, depending on time and interest. They can discuss it orally before comparing ideas with the class. Or they can spend more time on it and write out an ending, either in narrative or dialogue form. If it is a dialogue, it could be prepared in groups and acted out for the class.

PRONUNCIATION

1 ○ ● **Explanation**   Students get more practice in sentence stress and reading aloud. Getting the main stress right improves the fluency of a conversation and also understanding, as the information words are emphasized. Students need to get used to the idea that every sentence has a main stress which helps communication. If the sentence is long, there will be more than one word emphasized, usually the main word in each clause.

● **Practice**   Students refer back the story on page 81. They first work in pairs to try to work out the stress in each sentence. Then play the cassette for students to check their answers.

T.7.2
A

That was *good*.
The *director* didn't think so. *He* said he didn't want to *hear* my second piece.
Come and have a *coffee*. There's a place on the first *floor*.
Are you in *London* all the time now? Anna says she doesn't *see* you very often.
The *studios* are in London. When I have a few *free* days, I usually go up to Longthorpe *Castle* and see *Archie*.
Is *Anna* there when you go?
Anna? No, why *should* she be?
Oh, *no* reason. She spends a lot of *time* there, though. *I* think she's *keen* on Archie. I wonder if Archie's in *love* with her. What do *you* think?
Suzi, I don't *know* if Archie's in love with Anna. It's *their* business, not *yours*.

2 ○ ● **Explanation**   This exercise practises spelling and the sibilants /s/, /z/, /ʃ/.

● **Practice**   Work as a class. Put the sounds up on the board. Let the students say the sounds aloud and write the word in the correct column on the board. Discuss any problems.

A   /s/ rehearsal, close, suit, used to be, school, peaceful
/z/ films, reason, please, busy, excuse me, otherwise, housing
/ʃ/ audition, national, sugar, special, mushroom, conversion

3 ○ ● **Explanation**   Politeness is a matter of saying the right thing in the right context, in the right way. These examples are for discussion.

T.7.4
1 **Suzi** (friendly)	Hello, Sylvia. What are you doing here?
2 **Poppy** (rudely)	Hello, Sylvia What are *you* doing here?
3 **Registrar** (neutral)	Can I see your cards, please?
4 **Suzi** (anxious)	Don't you want to hear my other piece?
5 **Woman** (rudely)	No, thanks.
6 **Man** (politely)	No, thanks. That's fine.
7 **Staff** (reading list)	Yes, here you are . . .
8 **Tom** (breezily)	Here you are.

○ ● **Practice**   Play the cassette. Stop after each person. Discuss whether he/she is being polite, rude, or neutral.

Students can try to say the examples in different ways for different contexts, making them rude, polite, or neutral.

A   1P   2R   3N   4P   5R   6P   7N   8N

READING

○ ● **Explanation**   This text is a handout giving information about interviews and auditions. The auditions are for places in an orchestra and band.

○ ● **Warm-up**   Pre-teach some vocabulary:
vice versa   music stand   wind band
string section   modern jazz group

- **Practice**   Read the text in class. Make sure everyone understands. Ask the question in **1**, and then discuss the questions in **2**. Students can work in pairs to do exercise **3**.

A   1 Information
2   1 Places in an orchestra/wind band/modern jazz group
  2 One day
  3 In the afternoon
3   It's the details of the auditions for the music course/orchestra/wind band/modern jazz group. It tells me when it is, and how to get there. It gives me all the information I need for the day.

---

4 ○ ● **Explanation**   This is a vocabulary exercise that gives students a chance to practise explaining meanings in English.

● **Practice**   Students work in pairs to prepare explanations in English for each word.

A   *interview:* a meeting for asking some questions face to face
candidate: someone who is going to do an exam/audition for a place
car parking facilities: place where cars can be parked
packed lunch: sandwiches, etc. that you take with you
to be responsible for: to have to make your own arrangements; to be your duty to do something
in good time: not late

---

5 ○ ● **Explanation**   This is an optional translation exercise to test comprehension.

○ **Practice**   Students translate the paragraph into their own language, either orally around the class, or written as homework.

Options 7

ABOUT THE HOUSE

a ○ ● **Explanation**   When you are holidaying in a big house or hotel, you need to know the names of all the rooms and to be able to understand information about the 'geography' of the house. This exercise practises using and understanding the relevant vocabulary and phrases.

○ ● **Practice**   Students work alone or in pairs to match the pictures to the plan.

A   1 kitchen   3 dining room   5 bathroom
2 sitting room   4 bedroom B   6 bedroom A or C

---

b ○ ● Students work in pairs or small groups to find the meanings of the words and expressions. They can use their dictionaries to help them.

c ● Play the cassette while the students follow the directions through the house plan.

T.7.5   Go through the French windows into the sitting room. Go across the hall and up the stairs. Turn left at the top, and it's the last door on your right.

A   To bedroom C

● **Extension**   Students work in pairs to give each other directions through the house, as in the listening exercise.

DISCUSSION

a/b ○ ● **Explanation**   This is an oral fluency exercise which enables students to practise some of the vocabulary they have learnt in this unit.

● **Practice**   Students work in groups. First they discuss the type of film or play they would like to work on. Then they make decisions about the characters. They should have some idea about whether it will be amusing or serious to help them decide on the kind of actors they would need. Afterwards, each group can report to the rest of the class what their group decided.

● **Extension**   The groups can write the opening scene of their play or film and read or act it out for the class.

VOCABULARY

○ ● **Explanation**   Students identify the word that does not fit in each group and explain why.

● **Practice**   They can work alone, in pairs or in small groups to do this exercise, and then compare answers with the class.

A   *audition:* the others are all places where drama is performed
actor: the others are to do with drama, but are not people
car park: the others are all methods of transport
hear: the others are all to do with using the voice
garden: the others are all past participles

GRAMMAR

○ ● **Explanation**   *Say, tell*, and *talk* are often confused by foreign learners. We use *say* in a general way to describe using your voice to convey a message of some kind. We always *say something*. Whereas, *tell* is used to give another person information or an instruction and we usually *tell somebody something*. *Talk* implies two or more people having a conversation. We usually *talk to somebody about something*.

● **Practice**   Discuss the pictures and decide which one describes which verb. Then let students work in pairs to complete the sentences. Check answers as a class.

A   1 We *talked* about the weather.
2 John *said* it was a lovely day.
3 They were *talking* about politics.
4 She *told* me to hurry up.
5 Did you *hear* what she *said?*
6 Vera *told* Simon about the meeting.
7 They *said* they would lend me the money.

MESSAGES

○ ● **Explanation**   In this oral exercise students practise a form of reported speech.

● **Practice**   Students work in groups of four. Each group decides who is the 'difficult guest', and what role the other students will take. Then everybody sits in a circle. The difficult guest has to pass different sorts of messages to the people in the

house. The messages should go round the circle as quickly as possible. It should be fast and fun.

Students can use the examples provided, but encourage them to think of their own situations. They do not have to keep to the characters mentioned in the book.

COMMENTS

○ ● **Explanation**   This oral exercise can be used for pair work, group work, or in class. A lot of newspapers are needed to hand round. If each student can bring in a daily newspaper, so much the better.

● **Practice**   Each student can take on a role, e.g. a politician, a doctor, a teacher, a sportsman, and choose items that relate to that speciality. When Student A starts a conversation, Student B (and C and D, etc.) must make a further comment. If they cannot think of anything, they can start a new subject. The object is not to let conversation stop.

ENRICHMENT

○ ● **Explanation**   Students practise degrees with adjectives and comparatives. Also, particular adjectives are needed to describe size. Make sure, for example, that students do not say: *His shoes should be shorter*.

○ ● **Practice**   Students work in pairs to write their sentences. Then students compare their list with the rest of the class.

A   **Possible answers**
His hat is too small. It should be a bit bigger.
His jacket is much too small. It should be a lot bigger.
His trousers are too short. They should be much longer.
His shirt sleeves are too long. They should be much shorter.
His tie is much too long. It should be a lot shorter.
His shoes are much too big. They should be much smaller.
The bed is a bit narrow. It should be wider.
The door is too small. It should be a bit bigger.
The bedspread is much too big for the bed. It should be much smaller.
The carpet is much too small. It should be much bigger.

8
Preview

1 Second conditional

a ○ ● **Explanation** In Unit 5 we studied the first conditional: *if*+present tense+*will/won't*+verb, which we use to describe a possible or likely future happening, e.g. *If everybody helps, we'll finish the tidying up in an hour*. In this unit students are introduced to the second conditional: *if*+past tense+*would/wouldn't*+verb, which we use to describe a future situation which is hypothetical or unlikely to happen, e.g. *If I won a lot of money, I would travel round the world*. (The speaker doesn't really believe he/she will ever win a lot of money.)

T.8.1	**Young man**	If I saw a ghost, I'd scream.
	Woman	If I saw a ghost, I'd take a photograph of it.
	Girl	I'd climb under the table, if I saw a ghost.
	Boy	What would you do if the ghost were already under the table, eh?
	Woman 2	I'd invite it to supper.
	Man 2	No, you wouldn't. You'd run a mile!

○ ● **Practice** Play the cassette and let students hear and read what the people say. Discuss the questions as a class.

A 1 The tense of verb in the *if* clause is the past tense.
2 I'd = I would.
3 No, they don't think they are going to see a ghost.

b ● This exercise provides practice in manipulating the structure. Students work in pairs to complete the sentences, then compare their answers with the class.
Note The use of *were* for both singular and plural in the *if* clause instead of *was*, e.g. *If I **were** president, . . .* is the only remnant left of the English subjunctive which is otherwise the same as the past tense. However, it is now also acceptable to use *was*.

A **Possible answers**
1 If you cooked the dinner tonight, . . .
2 If I saw a snake, . . .
3 If I had the money, . . .
1 . . ., I would read more.
2 . . ., I'd travel.
3 . . ., I'd do more for the less privileged members of society.
4 . . ., I'd take you to the airport.

c ○ ● **Explanation** This exercise includes both first and second conditional sentences, so students must be careful with the tenses.

○ ● **Practice** Students work in pairs to match beginnings and endings to make appropriate sentences. They compare their answers with the class.

A 1d If I weren't so tired, I'd go to Jane's party. (*Hypothetical – I am tired.*)
2h If there isn't a green sweater in my size, I'll buy the blue one. (*Real – I will buy one of the jumpers.*)
3f If you had a car, you could drive to work. (*Hypothetical – You don't have a car.*)
4e If you cook dinner, I'll wash up. (*Real – We will have dinner.*)
5b If it weren't raining, I'd go out for a walk. (*Hypothetical – It is raining.*)
6g If they got married, it would be a disaster. (*Hypothetical – It is unlikely they will marry.*)
7c If it's fine tomorrow, we'll go to the beach. (*Real – We will go out tomorrow.*)
8a If Peter phones tonight, I'll go out with him. (*Real – It is possible that he'll phone.*)

Students discuss the questions about the use of the conditionals as a class. Look at each sentence and decide whether it is a real or a hypothetical situation, and why. Students can refer back to Unit 5 to refresh their memories. Write two headings on the board and fill in information about a) the first and b) the second conditional. Students can compare these structures with their own language, if it helps.

2   Superlative adjectives

- ○ ● **Explanation**   In Unit 2, students learnt the comparative form of adjectives. Students are now introduced to the superlative in the same way.

- ○ ● **Warm-up**   Use a few of the adjectives from the list. They are all known to students in their regular and comparative forms. Point to objects around the class and demonstrate the use of the different forms of the adjectives, e.g. *This is a thick book. This is a thicker book. This is the thickest book on the shelf. This pencil is longer than that pencil, but this pencil is the longest.*

- ○ ● **Practice**   Students work in pairs to fill in the superlative and sometimes comparative forms. They can use a dictionary to help them and should pay particular attention to spelling, which follows the same rules as for comparatives. Check answers as a class.

A

the smallest; the widest; the happiest; wetter/the wettest; thicker/the thickest; taller/the tallest; thinner/the thinnest; drier/the driest; more comfortable/the most comfortable; friendlier/the friendliest; more practical/the most practical; the best; the worst

3   Vocabulary

- ○ ● **Explanation**   Students sort out vocabulary related to holiday towns and buildings.

- ○ ● **Practice**   Students work in pairs or small groups to divide the words under the right headings. Some words fit both categories, some fit neither, but students should make sure they understand them all. Check answers as a class and make sure students pronounce the words correctly. They can use a dictionary to help them.

A

Holiday towns	Buildings	
castle	bathroom	haunted
luxury	passage	ghost
leisure park	castle	conversion
library	development	power cut
conference centre	conference centre	library

The following words do not really fall into either category: back(v), land, imagination, fuse(n), chilly.

Things that go bump in the night

T.8.2   Poppy and Max are staying with Archie at Longthorpe Castle. They are in a room in a very old part of the castle and Poppy wonders if the castle is haunted. Sylvia is also at the castle, and Archie talks to her about his plans for the castle; he hopes Max is going to back him. Archie wants to set up a leisure park and hotel so that he can go on living at the castle. Sylvia is surprised when Toby arrives at tea time – she had not known he was coming. Archie has asked Toby to do the conversion work on the castle.

After dinner, Toby shows everyone the plans he has drawn up. Max likes them a lot. Poppy does too, but she is more interested in finding out whether the castle is haunted. Archie's mother has always said that the room they are in is haunted and she will not stay in it alone after dark. Suddenly, they hear a noise, the temperature in the room drops, all the lights go out, and they see something moving . . .

The people in this episode

Poppy loves being at the castle, surrounded by all the lovely old furniture. She makes her usual forthright comments. She seems most interested in ghosts and haunting, and talks about them to Max, and then Archie.

Max does not believe in ghosts. He is there on business and as a friend. As usual, he is polite and urbane, although he is ruffled by Poppy's behaviour. He is impressed by Toby's work, especially because he fired him from his own firm.

Archie is a good host and at ease with his sister and friends. He knows that Toby's presence might be awkward for Sylvia, but clearly at the moment, his plans for the castle are his chief concern.

Sylvia is at home in the castle, although she is Archie's step-sister, and it is not her family home. She is very interested in Archie's plans, and does not make an issue of Toby's presence, though she is surprised.

Toby feels a little awkward when he meets Sylvia again. He greets her quickly and then heads for tea. He, too, is going to make his work on the castle his main reason for being there.

● **Warm-up**   Look at the picture. Ask:

Who is there?
Where are they?
Why are they there?
Are they all having a friendly conversation, or is something wrong?

Play the cassette of the whole episode.

Now play the cassette again, section by section. Ask questions about each section:

Where are they?
Who's talking to whom?
What are they talking about?
Does anything striking happen?

Ask check questions like these:

What do Max and Poppy talk about?
What are Archie's plans?
Did Sylvia know that Toby was coming?
Do Toby and Sylvia feel uncomfortable about meeting there?
Who says the room is haunted?
What happens in the room?

Ask the students:

Is there a ghost?
How will the characters react?
What do you think will happen next?

Performance 8

COMPREHENSION

○ ● **Explanation**   These are quick check questions on the text.

○ ● **Practice**   Work as a class to say whether the statements are true or false.

A

1 True	5 True	9 True
2 False	6 True	10 True
3 False	7 False	11 False
4 True	8 False	12 False

PRACTICE

1 ○ ● **Explanation**   This exercise practises second conditionals using hypothetical situations.

● **Practice**   Students work in pairs. They ask and answer the questions using the second conditional form: *if* + past tense + *would(not)* + verb. Each person describes to the class what his/her partner would do.

2 ○ ● **Explanation**   This is written practice, filling in the right forms of the verbs.

○ ● **Practice**   Students work alone or in pairs to do the exercise. They check their answers with the rest of the class.

A

If I were the Minister of Transport, **I'd make** public transport cheaper than it is now. If fares **were** less expensive, more people **would use** buses and the Underground. If more people **used** public transport, it **would be** very crowded, so **I'd increase** the number of trains and buses and **I'd ban** cars from the city centre. If there **weren't** any cars in the centre, there **would be** less traffic and the buses could **go** faster than they do now. There **would be** less pollution and everybody **would be** healthier!

3 ○ ● **Explanation**   Here is further practice in conditionals, choosing the correct tenses of the verbs.

○ ● **Practice**   Let students work in small groups so they can talk about appropriate answers. They can compare their answers with the rest of the class.

1 **Poppy**   If I **wanted** a lot of bathrooms, I **wouldn't live** in a castle.
2 **Poppy**   But if you **saw** a real ghost, Max, you**'d believe** in them.
3 **Max**   If you **saw** a ghost, you **wouldn't scream**, you**'d say** 'Don't be silly.'
4 **Archie**   But if I **did** that, I couldn't live here.
5 **Archie**   If they **turned** it into a hotel, **I'd hate** it.
6 **Archie**   She**'d die** if she **had to** sleep in it.

4a○ ● **Explanation**   Only one of the three plans fits with what Archie says in the story.

○ ● **Practice**   Students discuss the plans from what they can remember of the soap. Then play the cassette from Sylvia's words: *Is Max going to back your plans?* to *Here's Toby*, so that students can check their ideas. Plan C is the one Archie likes. Ask the students if they agree with Archie's choice, or if they themselves prefer another one.

b ○ ● **Explanation**   Students make conditional sentences to explain the consequences of the three plans. They look first at the example sentences. A and B are the most unlikely so the second conditional is used. Plan C is the most likely, so the first conditional is used here.

● **Practice**   Students can work in pairs or as a class. They will need to organize the information to make appropriate sentences.

Possible answers

Plan A   . . . If he built houses, he could sell them and make a lot of money.
   If he made enough money, he could live in the castle.

Plan B   If Archie sold the castle and the land, someone else would turn it into a hotel or conference centre.
   If Archie sold the castle, he would have to live somewhere else.

Plan C   . . . If Archie repairs the castle, Max and Archie will turn part of it into a luxury hotel.
   If Archie turns the castle into a luxury hotel, he can live in the west wing.

5 ○ ● **Explanation**   In this listening task, students have to decide whether the two people are keen on an idea or not. They may need to listen several times. The answers are not given explicitly and students may find it difficult to explain why or why not.

● **Practice**   Play the cassette through once. The students then discuss the answers in pairs. Play the cassette as many times as necessary for the students to fill in all the answers.

T.8.3   **Woman**   What about the zoo idea?
   Man   A small zoo . . . perhaps. What kind of a zoo, though?
   Woman   Not lions and tigers. That's dangerous.
   Man   Yes, and people don't like to see wild animals in zoos nowadays.
   Woman   We could have baby animals, ponies, that kind of thing, for the children.
   Man   Possibly, but I think you need a lot of extra staff for that.
   Woman   That's true. Not a good idea. Hotel?
   Man   No. It's not going to be possible to get planning permission.
   Woman   In any case, it's an expert job, running a hotel.
   Man   I like the idea of a swimming pool.
   Woman   Yes, but it would have to be something special. And indoor pools are very expensive.
   Man   Mmm. In a few years' time, perhaps.
   Woman   I agree. Now, I like the steam railway idea.
   Man   So do I. That's always popular. We'll have to be careful about safety, though. Have you thought of a route?
   Woman   George is making a plan for it.
   Man   And I also think the adventure playground is a good idea.
   Woman   Oh, yes. You have to have an adventure playground these days.

Zoo: No. Lions and tigers are dangerous, and people do not like to see wild animals in zoos. Also, you need a lot of staff for the younger animals.
Hotel: No. Cannot get planning permission, and it is a job for experts.
Swimming pool: Maybe, in a few years' time. It would have to be something special. And they are expensive.
Steam railway: Yes. They are popular.
Playground: Yes. They are very fashionable.

6a○ ● **Explanation**   One of the main uses of the second conditional is to express a hypothetical condition and its result. The condition is hypothetical because the speaker believes it to be highly unlikely or even improbable. The use of the first conditional describes a real condition and its result. Often the choice of tense only depends on whether the speaker *believes* the condition to be a real or hypothetical one. In **a**, students have to work this out; in **b** they have to produce their own sentences to demonstrate it.

○ ● **Practice**   Read the two examples. Ask:

Is the sentence in the first or second conditional?
Does the speaker believe this could actually happen?

Students then work in pairs to discuss whether the sentences are real or hypothetical. Discuss the answers as a class, and the situation of the speaker which makes the conditions real or hypothetical.

A

1 real (She must be considering a job offer in Hawaii.)
2 real (They are considering their holiday choices.)
3 hypothetical (I always do my homework.)
4 real (I am considering lending you my Walkman.)
5 hypothetical (I don't expect to see any mice in my house.)
6 hypothetical (You don't expect anyone to give you compliments.)

b   ● Students now produce their own sentences using the appropriate conditional to show if the situation is real or hypothetical. The students must make sensible choices – some of the situations could be both real or hypothetical depending on opinion, others are more obviously hypothetical. Students work in pairs to make their sentences. They compare their answers as a class.

A

see a ghost

hypothetical:	run away.
If I saw a ghost, I'd	scream.
	laugh.

live on a desert island

hypothetical:	be very lonely.
If I lived on a desert island, I'd	try to escape.
	build a boat.

dye hair pink

real:	my mother will be shocked.
If I dye my hair pink,	people will stare.
	my teacher will be angry.

hypothetical:	my mother would be shocked.
If I dyed my hair pink,	people would stare.
	my teacher would be angry.

have lots of money

real:	buy a castle.
If/When I have lots of money, I'll	go round the world.
hypothetical:	
If I had lots of money, I'd	drive a big car.

car break down

real:	walk.
If the car breaks down, I'll	call a taxi.
hypothetical:	
If the car broke down, I'd	cry.

7○ ● **Explanation**   This exercise practises superlatives. Students find a noun that can be described by the adjective and then make a noun phrase using the superlative form, as in the example.

● **Practice**   Students work in pairs. The points to be most careful about are:
a) spelling of the superlative form
b) appropriacy of adjective and noun match.

Compare answers as a class.

A   **Sample answers**
small: the smallest kitten in the litter
wide: the widest part of the river
happy: the happiest baby I know
wet: the wettest day this year
thick: the thickest blanket in the house
tall: the tallest person in my family
thin: the thinnest slice of cake you can cut
dry: the driest piece of bread you can imagine
expensive: the most expensive jacket in the shop
comfortable: the most comfortable chair in the room
friendly: the friendliest person in my street
practical: the most practical present I can think of
good: the best result in the class
bad: the worst marks in the class

8a ○ ● **Explanation**   Here is more practice in superlatives. The objects are all clearly associated with the characters from past episodes. Make clear to students that these objects are in some way special in the lives of the characters.

● **Practice**   In pairs or as a class, discuss which object fits each character. Students can look through earlier episodes to help them.

> **A**   Max: building; Anna: seriously-ill patient; Poppy: dress; Toby: armchair; Sylvia: tape recorder; Archie: sports car

b ● Students work in groups to produce sentences using the nouns and adjectives from **a**, as in the example. The groups compare answers.

> **A**   **Possible answers**
> That's Archie's fastest sports car.
> That's Poppy's prettiest dress.
> That's Sylvia's best machine for her job.
> That's Toby's most comfortable chair.
> That's Anna's most difficult case.

c ● This is a free exercise to practise superlatives, based on the vocabulary in **a** and **b** and the additional adjectives listed, although students can make their own choice. Students use the example in their book as a model. They should take a few minutes to think about what they want to talk about, make up a superlative sentence about it, and then work in pairs. When they have each correctly guessed why the objects are special, they can change pairs and repeat the exercise.

9 ○ ● **Explanation**   This exercise also practises superlatives. Students have to study the track from the viewpoint of the drivers and spectators. You can put up further vocabulary to help them, e.g. *corner, accidents, straight section, track*.

● **Practice**   Students work in small groups to do the exercise. Then they compare their sentences with other groups.

> **A**   2 This is the most dangerous corner.
> 3 This is the best place to watch the race.
> 4 This is the narrowest part of the track.
> 5 This is the longest straight section of the track.
> 6 This is the widest part of the track.
> 7 This is the the steepest part of the track.
> 8 This is the worst place for accidents.

● **Extension**   Students can write a report from a racing driver about 'Why I hate/love driving on this track.'

PRONUNCIATION

1 ○ ● **Explanation**   This is a practice exercise in word stress.

● **Practice**   Read out the list of words. Let students work in pairs to underline the main stress in each word. Alternatively, one student in a pair reads the words out, while the other student marks down the stress made. When they have both done this, they can compare their pronunciation of the words. Check pronunciation as a class.

> **A**
>
> | conference | by herself | conversion |
> | somebody | luxury | anywhere |
> | passage | facilities | library |
> | development | half an hour ago | programme |
> | audition | rehearsal | director |
> | modern | corridor | I think so |
> | impossible | registration | |

2 ○ ● **Explanation**   Students have to listen to the stress and intonation and decide which pronunciation better suits the situation in the picture. Students might like to suggest what was previously said in each case, e.g. *Do you take this woman for your lawful wedded wife?/I do.*

> **T.8.4**
> 1 a I do. (emphatic)
>   b I do. (wedding)
> 2 a Do you mind? (indignant)
>   b Do you mind? (calm)
> 3 a What are you doing? (normal question)
>   b What are you doing? (indignant, horrified)
> 4 a I didn't eat any cake. (normal sentence)
>   b I didn't eat any cake. (in self defence)

● **Practice**   Students study the pictures and try to imagine how the words in the speech bubbles are spoken. Play the cassette. Stop after each pair of sentences. Let students discuss in pairs which is the correct one and write down their answer, **a** or **b**. Play the cassette again for the whole class and discuss the answers.

> **A**   1b   2a   3b   4b

3 ○ ● **Explanation**   The short /ɪ/ sound is one of the most commonly mispronounced for various reasons: a) at the end of a word (e.g. in *money*) it is taught as a long /iː/, which is not very common in everyday connected speech; b) if the word is written with 'i', students tend to make it long, as in *facilities*, c) it is sometimes written with letters that look quite different, e.g. *passage*.
Elsewhere, students sometimes say /ɪ/ instead of /aɪ/ when they see the 'i' spelling, e.g. in *mind*.

● **Practice**   Students work in pairs to underline the /ɪ/ sounds. First read out the lists of words to the students. They can use their dictionaries to help them and to check their answers.

A   anywhere   money   lovely   passage   find
library   believe   minute   development
keep   build   facilities   live   building
mind   family   friend   dinner   haunted
imagination   skidded   crashed

READING

○ ● **Explanation**   This text is a complete short ghost story, written in the early fifties. What is the 'twist' at the end that makes it a good short story?

○ ● **Practice**   Students read the story by themselves. Ask a few students to explain what it is about. Discuss the 'twist in the story' as a class. Let the students answer the questions in pairs and compare their answers with the rest of the class afterwards.

A   1 The narrator is a woman in her late forties/a middle-aged woman. She is unmarried, lives alone, and is a teacher. She has dark hair and is short-sighted.
2 The other person is a young man of about twenty. He has long curly hair, blue eyes, and a firm nose and chin. He does not look very well, but dresses in striking clothes. He is a writer.
3 A ghost story./A short story.
4 Christmas Day.
5 Both characters.
7 It is written in the present simple and present perfect. This makes the past seem much closer to the present.
8 So she was relieved when the young man walked in. There was nothing romantic about it – she was

a woman of nearly fifty, a spinster schoolmistress with dark hair and short-sighted eyes that once were beautiful. He was around twenty, dressed in a black velvet jacket and a flowing, wine-coloured tie. His hair was long and he had brown curls. He had narrow, piercing blue eyes and a firm nose and chin. He didn't look strong. He burst in without knocking, then paused and said he was sorry. He had thought it was his room. He began to go out, then hesitated and asked if she was alone.

Options 8

ENRICHMENT

○ ● **Explanation**   The people in the pictures are thoroughly miserable, and the student's job is to make as many helpful/sympathetic suggestions as possible. Students can use *should*, or the useful phrase *what you need is . . . .*

● **Practice**   Discuss the situations as a class and let students suggest why the person in the picture is feeling absolutely fed up. Write the details on the board, then ask students to come up with helpful suggestions. The rest of the class says whether it is a useful or an unhelpful suggestion.

A   **Possible answers**
1 What you need is a scarf, hat, and gloves.
2 What you need is a suitcase.
3 What you need is an electric typewriter/a word processor.
4 You should use a calculator.

● **Extension**   The other main function of the second conditional is to offer advice: *If I were you/her, I'd wear a warm scarf and a woolly hat.* Students use the best advice offered in the exercises to make second conditional sentences as above.

VOCABULARY

○ ● **Explanation**   Students have to find the regular and irregular comparative forms in the word square and then write its superlative form. They will find the seventeen answers going down and across.

● **Practice**   Students do the exercise alone or in pairs and compare answers.

```
C  P  W  L  R  S  P  A  L  E  R  E  B  Z  I
S  M  P  M  X  I  R  V  H  A  P  P  I  E  R
O  W  W  O  R  S  E  K  W  M  P  A  G  S  M
D  P  M  R  T  H  I  C  K  E  R  L  G  N  O
M  O  R  E  E  X  P  E  N  S  I  V  E  Y  R
H  O  E  F  C  L  T  W  I  D  E  R  R  E  E
S  C  O  R  Z  A  H  U  C  S  P  K  N  U  U
M  O  T  I  S  I  I  B  E  T  T  E  R  N  S
A  U  K  E  S  L  N  M  P  R  A  S  O  Y  E
L  E  B  N  L  O  N  G  E  R  L  P  L  K  F
L  H  R  D  R  I  E  R  O  U  L  O  D  N  U
E  C  S  L  G  D  R  A  P  Z  E  C  E  M  L
R  E  G  Y  S  W  E  T  T  E  R  G  R  W  K
```

Across

paler	palest
happier	happiest
worse	worst
thicker	thickest
more expensive	most expensive
wider	widest
better	best
longer	longest
drier	driest
wetter	wettest

Down

smaller	smallest
more friendly	most friendly*
thinner	thinnest
taller	tallest
bigger	biggest
older	oldest
more useful	most useful

*(also friendlier/friendliest)

REVISION

○ ● **Explanation**   Punctuation is much easier if students know what each mark represents, but regular revision is required. The structures concerned are all very basic, but correct punctuation is highly valued by employers and is therefore worth getting right. The exercise continues practice which began in Book 1.

Thus use of 's to mean *has* usually indicates speech or the written form of speech. Note the plural possessive in number 10.

● **Practice**   Students work in pairs to write the apostrophes and identify what they represent. Discuss the answers as a class.

1 He's (has)
2 She's (is), St John's (possessive)
3 He's (is), friend's (possessive), at Romeo's (possessive)
4 He's (has)
5 It's (is), Max's (possessive)
6 Archie's (possessive), castle's (has)
7 Your wife's (has), she's (is)
8 There's (is)
9 There's (has), Tom's (possessive)
10 Suzi's (possessive), Suzi's (is), parents' (plural possessive)
11 Toby's (has)
12 She's (has), Anna's (possessive), disk's (is)

READING FOR INFORMATION

Information about tickets

○ ● **Explanation**   Reading for information usually means reading quickly, because the eye learns to ignore the information which is *not* required.

● **Practice**   Students work alone and then check their answers in pairs or small groups. Remind the students that it is price per kilometre.

1 The Christmas Shopper
2 A cheap day return
3 A blue saver
4 A white saver
5 An ordinary return
6 A single

READING

- ○ ● **Explanation**   This is a puzzle and an exercise in cultural understanding.

- ○ ● **Practice**   Students work in pairs. They have to read the texts and put the names in the right places. It is not necessary for them to understand every word to do the exercise. Students should read the whole text through and start with the obvious pairs, e.g. General Post Office/GPO. It may take a little time. Discuss the answers as a class.

A   The **Mansion House** has been the Lord Mayor's residence since 1715.
The **Four Courts** is where the Supreme and High Courts sit.
The **Custom House** dates from 1791. All goods coming into the city by river had to come through here.
The **City Hall** has been the headquarters of the city administration since 1852.
The **Bank of Ireland** used to be the Irish Parliament House. It is a normal bank. You can change money here if you wish.
The **General Post Office** is known as the GPO. The Proclamation of the Irish Republic was read here during the Easter Rising in 1916.
Leinster House was the eighteenth-century home of the Dukes of Leinster. The Irish Parliament now sits here.

SMALL TALK

- ○ ● **Explanation**   This is an exercise in making conversation and includes practice of comparatives and superlatives. Towns are quite a useful subject with people you do not know. As a class, make a list of helpful negative and positive adjectives on the board (see below). You can also write a list of towns, and give them a rating (1–10) for each adjective. Rate other features: best restaurants, worst swimming, most expensive shops, etc.

  Useful adjectives: *lively, expensive, interesting, historic, romantic, boring, hilly, busy, dirty, old, noisy, stimulating, exciting.*

- ● **Practice**   Students work in pairs to practise dialogues. They can either treat the exercise as oral fluency practice, or prepare and write their dialogues first.

9
Preview

1 Past continuous

○ ● **Explanation** This exercise introduces the form of the past continuous tense.

● **Practice** Ask students to complete the table and work out the new tense for themselves. They can write the correct forms of the present and past continuous on the board to check.

A		**Present continuous**	**Past continuous**
	Negative	She isn't talking.	She wasn't talking.
	Question	Is she talking?	Was she talking?

2 *-ing* forms

○ ● **Explanation** Students identify the different uses of the *-ing* form: noun, adjective, present continuous to describe an action happening now or in the future, or past continuous.

○ ● **Practice** Read the sentences as a class. The students work in small groups to tick the correct column. Discuss the answers as a class.

A	Pres. cont.	Pres. cont. as future	Past cont.	Noun	Adj
1	✓				
2		✓			
3			✓		
4				✓	
5			✓		
6	✓				
7				✓	
8					✓
9		✓			
10					✓

3 Future time

○ ● **Explanation** Students have learnt the structure of the first conditional with *if* for possible future events, e.g. *If I get married, I'll buy a house*, and have been introduced to *when* for certain future events, e.g. *When I get married, I'll buy a house*. Here, students look again at sentences with *when*, and are introduced to negative sentences with *until*. Remind students that the future time clause with *if, when, until* is in the present tense.

○ ● **Practice** Students study the sentences in pairs and answer the questions themselves first. Then ask them to explain what they have discovered. If the students are unclear, read the first sentence. Ask students: *What time is the person talking about – the past, present or future?*

Read the other sentences. Ask:

Which two tenses are there in each sentence?
Which tense is used in the main clause?
*Which tense is used in the **when/until** clause?*
*What happens in the main clause with an **until** clause?*

Students discuss how this structure compares to their own language. Then they work in pairs to translate the four sentences.

4 *must/mustn't*

○ ● **Explanation** The pictures introduce students to the main use of *must/mustn't* as a way of giving orders or instructions by people in authority. Students tend to overuse *must* instead of using *have to* for general obligation, therefore it should be made clear that *must* is usually a command.

Practice   As a class, decide who is talking to who in each picture. In pairs, students decide on the general function of *must*. Discuss the answers as a class and refer to the Grammar Summary on page 109 for the answers.

A	1 doctor talking to patient
	2 man talking to himself
	3 teacher talking to student
	4 management talking to clients

In general, these are all figures of authority speaking, and who are therefore allowed to give orders/instructions. Number 2 is an idiomatic exception, but can be seen as the person giving an order to himself.

5   Vocabulary

Explanation   Students identify the words that relate to weddings.

Practice   Read the list of words to the students and let them practise the pronunciation of those they do not know. Then students work in pairs to find those words that have to do with weddings. They can use their dictionaries to help them. Students share their answers as a class and discuss the meanings.

A	bouquet marry Registry Office groom
	witness bride

6   *too . . ./not . . . enough*

Explanation   Students have already met the structure *too*+adjective in Options 7. They are now introduced to the negative version *not*+adjective+*enough*.

Practice   Students work in pairs to study the pictures at the bottom of the page and write one sentence describing each picture, using *not . . . enough*. Afterwards, students compare the answers in class.

A	1 The seat is not big enough (for them).
	2 The light is not bright enough (for him).
	3 The child is not tall enough.
	4 The water is not warm enough (for him).
	5 The car is not big enough (for them all).

Wedding bells

T.9.1   It is Anna and Archie's wedding day. It is rather chaotic at Lion Place where Anna, Suzi, and Sylvia are getting ready. While Anna is rushing round making last minute calls to the hospital, Sylvia is helping Suzi into her dress. Suzi tells Sylvia that she got the part in the film and is off to America after the National Youth Theatre (NYT) season has finished. Sylvia is very pleased for Suzi but warns her that she will not necessarily become rich and successful overnight.

Eventually, Suzi and Sylvia manage to persuade Anna to stop thinking about work and get to the Registry Office. On the way they talk about the age difference between Anna and Archie (two years) and between Poppy and Max (22 years). Suzi says she only wants to get married when she is thirty and then to someone her own age. They arrive only just in time – the official is about to lock up because he thinks they are not coming. After some confusion about who is the groom, the wedding gets started.

The people in this episode

Anna is clearly as disorganized in her private life as she is organized and controlled at work. Less than an hour before her wedding, she is still running around tying her bouquet. She was at work till midnight the night before and is still concerned about what is happening at the hospital. She is not nervous though, and finds time to joke with her sister about her (Suzi's) ideas on getting married.

Suzi is as usual more interested in her own life than the things going on around her. She is concerned about the time, though and tries to hurry Anna up. She is dreaming of becoming an instant star.

Sylvia remains calm and down-to-earth with the chaos around her. She talks sensibly to Suzi while helping her get dressed and warns her not to expect instant success. She reminds Anna that this is her wedding day and work can wait.

Max is surprised that the bride is late and jokes that he is glad Anna is not his doctor.

Archie sounds calm. He obviously expected Anna to be late, showing that he knows, understands, and accepts his new wife-to-be's virtues and failings.

Tom in his usual muddling way allows the official to think he is the groom, which held the Registry Office open long enough for everyone to gather.

- **Warm-up**   Look at the picture. Ask:

Who are the people?
Where are they?
What do you think is happening?
Do they look happy? excited? nervous? confused?

Play the cassette. Ask:

Where are Sylvia, Anna, and Suzi?
What are they doing?
Why must they hurry?
Where are Max, Archie, and Tom?
What are they waiting for?

Play the cassette again. Stop after each section and ask check questions, e.g.

Why is Suzi on a diet?
What is she going to do in America?
Is Anna organized? How do you know?
Is Archie worried because Anna's late?
Why wouldn't Max want Anna as his doctor?
What time is the wedding supposed to be?

Performance 9

COMPREHENSION

1 ○ ● **Explanation**   Students complete the sentences with information from the text.

- **Warm-up**   Ask students to describe the main events in this episode. Do this by asking them to think of each of the characters; what they say, do, are going to do, or have done. Then discuss as a class.

○ ● **Practice**   Students work in groups to complete the sentences, if possible, without looking back at the story. They compare their answers as a class.

A   **Possible answers**
 1 Suzi can't do her dress up.
 2 Suzi is on a diet because she's going to America to be in a film.
 3 Suzi wants to be a star.
 4 Anna isn't in her room.
 5 She's downstairs, in the kitchen.
 6 Anna was running down the stairs, and she dropped her bouquet.
 7 Anna wants to ring Dr Greyson.

 8 Last night, Anna worked at the hospital until midnight.
 9 Archie is two years older than Anna.
10 Suzi wants to get married when she's thirty.
11 Anna's private life is disorganized.
12 The Registry Office closes at four.
13 The official let Tom in because he thought Tom was the groom.

2 ○ ● **Explanation**   This is a vocabulary exercise. Students use the context to help them work out the meaning of the words and phrases.

○ ● **Practice**   Students work in groups to work out the answers. If they have difficulties, they can use their dictionaries. They compare their answers as a class.

A   *on a diet:* following an eating programme that will help her lose some weight
the NYT season: the programme of plays fixed over a period of time by the National Youth Theatre group
shooting: the filming
be a star: be famous and successful as an actor/actress
until midnight last night: until twelve o'clock the night before
someone my own age: a person who is the same age as you
waiting for her to turn up: waiting for her to arrive
disorganized: not able to organize things in her life efficiently
the witnesses: the people who watch the wedding take place and sign their names to say that they have seen it happen
You're sure about that?: Are you certain that you are right?

3 ○ ● **Explanation**   This is a vocabulary lesson on personality adjectives and also asks students to discuss the characters of the people in the story.

○ ● **Warm-up**   Read the words and let the students practise saying them. They can use their dictionaries to help them find the meanings.

- **Practice**   Students work in pairs to decide on the answers using evidence from the episode. Discuss the answers. Students should explain why the person can be described in that way.

A **Possible answers**

helpful: Sylvia helps Suzi dress and gives her advice.

unpunctual: Anna is well-known for always being late outside her work.

tactless: Suzi is always being tactless. She says what is on her mind, without thinking about how this affects or criticizes others.

hard-working: Anna is hard-working. She worked till midnight on the eve of her wedding.

impatient: Suzi is impatient – many people are when it is not they who are busy/preoccupied. Max is also impatient; he hates waiting for people – especially if they are late.

relaxed: Archie seems relaxed. He knows Anna will arrive eventually.

quick-witted: Tom lets the official think he is the groom to stop him locking the office.

cross: The offical is angry about people not arriving in time for the wedding.

PRACTICE

1 ○ ● **Explanation**   This exercise practises the use of the past continuous. It can be done as a memory game. Students look at the picture for a short time, then close their books and try to remember what each of the people were doing when the fire alarm went off.

Note   The past continuous here describes actions in progress for some time until they are stopped by a new action, i.e. *the fire alarm went off.*

○ ● **Practice**   Students study the picture for no more than a minute. Then they close their books and say what each person was doing. Ask questions like *What was Mark doing?* if necessary. Students can disagree with other students' answers and try to correct them. Then they look back at the picture to check their answers.

A **Possible answers**

When the fire alarm went off, . . .

　　Mark was hanging up his coat.
　　Jane was working on the computer.
　　Roger was pouring a cup of coffee.
　　Penny was writing a letter.
　　George was taking something out of a drawer.

2a○ ● **Explanation**   This is a listening and speaking exercise using the past continuous, based on a murder story.

● **Practice**   The chart lists the ten people who were at the house when the murder took place. Students read the list of names and clues and try to identify each character in the picture. Encourage the students to use *must be* and *can't be* to make deductions, as in Options 8. Students compare answers before doing **b**.

b ● Students listen to the tape and fill in the chart on page 105 to note where each person says he/she was at seven o'clock that evening, and what they were doing. Play the cassette a second time so students can check their answers.

T.9.2		
1	Police	Where were you at seven o'clock, Mr Smith?
	Zachary	I was in the library.
	Police	What were you doing there?
	Zachary	I was reading a book.
2	Police	You're James Fenley?
	James	Yes.
	Police	What were you doing at seven o'clock?
	James	I was having a bath.
	Police	So you were in the bathroom?
	James	Yes.
3	Police	What were you doing, Mrs Spoon?
	Mrs Spoon	I was cooking dinner.
4	Police	Were you in the kitchen, too, Mr Croft?
	Mr Croft	No, I was answering the phone in the hall.
5	Lily	I'm Lily Goddard. I was watering the plants in the conservatory.
6	Felicity	This is ridiculous.
	Police	You're Felicity Fenley.
	Felicity	That's right. Where was I? In the attic, painting.
7	Lady Fenley	Oh dear, this is terrible.
	Police	Please sit down, Lady Fenley. We want to know where you were at seven, and what you were doing.
	Lady Fenley	Seven? Let me think . . . I was in the sitting room. I was listening to the radio.
8	Mrs Trim	I don't know anything about this.
	Police	Were you in your room at seven o'clock, Mrs Trim?
	Mrs Trim	No, I wasn't. I was looking for my glasses in the dining room.
9	Police	You're Sir Hugh's cousin, are you?

Henry	Yes. I'm staying here for a few days.
Police	Where were you at seven?
Henry	Oh, I was in my room. I was lying down – tired, you know. The country is very tiring.
10 **Police**	Sir Hugh, were you in your study all evening?
Sir Hugh	I think so . . . Let me see, yes. I was working. I'm writing a book . . . Yes, I was in the study.

A

Zachary Smith: library
James Fenley: bathroom
Mrs Spoon: kitchen
Mr Croft: hall
Lily Goddard: conservatory
Felicity Fenley: attic
Lady Fenley: sitting room
Mrs Trim: dining room
Henry: his bedroom
Sir Hugh Fenley: his study

c ● Students now check their chart and the picture that shows where each of the characters really were at seven o'clock. Students work in pairs to ask and answer about each person as in the example. One student uses the chart to ask questions, the other student uses the picture to answer as in the example. Students mark the chart to show if the person was telling the truth.

A

Zachary Smith: in the library sleeping, not reading
Lady Fenley: in the sitting room listening to the radio
Mrs Trim: in the dining room looking for her glasses
Mrs Spoon: not in the kitchen cooking, in the hall on the phone
Mr Croft: not answering the phone, reading the paper in the kitchen
Sir Hugh: not in his study working, but coming into house via back door
Lily Goddard and Cousin Henry: in attic together, so she wasn't in the conservatory watering the plants and he wasn't in his bedroom lying down
James and Felicity: in the conservatory arguing, so he wasn't in the bathroom having a bath, and she wasn't in the attic painting.

d ○ ● In groups, students now discuss who was lying and why. They discuss the four questions. Each group then makes up its own version of what happened and who killed Roland. Then the groups compare answers as a class, and hear the other groups' stories.

A **Possible answers**

1 *Zachary Smith, Lady Fenley, Mrs Trim* were telling the truth about where they were, and what they were doing, except that it seems *Zachary Smith*, as he is always tired, fell asleep while reading his book.

2 *Mrs Spoon* lied to cover up for the butler who was relaxing in the kitchen, or because she was using the phone without permission.
Mr Croft lied because he was not working as he should have been, or because he was covering up the fact that he saw *Sir Hugh* coming in the back door.
Lily Goddard and *Cousin Henry* lied because they are having a secret affair.
James and *Felicity* lied, but they had no reason to lie about where they were and what they were doing, unless they had been involved in the murder. The conservatory is beside the garden.
Sir Hugh also lied because he was coming in from the garden at seven, but it is also possible he was simply taking a breath of fresh air while working, saw and recognized the murderer, and was covering this up.

3 *James, Felicity*, and *Sir Hugh* are the likely suspects.

4 The students can make up any story about why one or all three of them did the murder and how it happened. A possible scenario could be: *Roland*, the ex-boyfriend, was blackmailing *Sir Hugh* and *Felicity* about his relationship with *Felicity*. As he is an undesirable character and *Felicity* was secretly still seeing him throughout her engagement to *Zachary*, this would prevent her marriage to the rich *Zachary*. *Sir Hugh* and *Felicity* therefore called *Roland* to a secret meeting and *Sir Hugh* shot him either in cold blood or in anger. *James* found out about the plan and argued with *Felicity* about it.

3a ○ ● **Explanation** This exercise practises *must/mustn't* as a way of expressing an obligation to oneself, giving oneself orders.

● **Practice** Students in pairs write what Archie tells himself he *must do/mustn't forget to do* before his wedding.

A **Possible answers**
I must confirm the honeymoon hotel.
I must get my suit dry-cleaned.
I mustn't forget to have my hair cut.
I mustn't forget to set my alarm clock.
I must have the car checked.
I must get to the Registry Office before four.
I mustn't forget the ring!

---

b ● When we write messages for ourselves, e.g. in a diary, it is usually enough just to write a name (and time). Students practise writing and interpreting short messages using *must/mustn't*. First, students write 3–4 short messages like the ones in **a**. Then they work in pairs to interpret one another's messages as in the example.

4a ○ ● **Explanation** This exercise practises the use of the present simple tense in time clauses after *when* or *until* to talk about future events.

○ ● **Practice** Students work in pairs to prepare sentences about what David and Sarah *will do* when they are a particular age. Encourage students to add their own ideas to the list. Discuss the answers.

b ● Look at the example with the students and practise making questions with the prompts first. Then students work in pairs to talk about their own lives, using the same structures. Afterwards students can report back to the class what their partner has said, e.g. *. . . says he/she will not leave school until he/she has passed the university entrance exam.*

5a ○ ● **Explanation** This is an oral fluency exercise to practise the vocabulary of weddings. It also gives students an opportunity to compare cultural differences with regard to weddings.

○ ● **Warm-up** Before students look at the flow chart, revise wedding vocabulary from the unit and pre-teach further new vocabulary: *to get engaged, priest, reception, honeymoon.*

● **Practice** Students work in pairs. They take turns to study the chart and then, with the book closed, tell their partner what happens at each stage. Ask how much they were able to remember. Alternatively, this can be done as a class exercise with students adding information one at a time around the class.

b ○ ● **Explanation** Students work with a partner again or in groups to draw up a similar chart to describe the stages a wedding would go through in their own country.

○ ● **Practice** Students describe what it is like in their own country, either orally to an imaginary English friend, or in a letter to an English friend. Students should say how traditions differ between the two countries. The letter can be done for homework.

6 ○ ● **Explanation** This is an oral fluency exercise where students have the opportunity to compare weddings in other cultures.

○ ● **Practice** Students look at the pictures of weddings and guess which country each of the weddings is from.

A 1 Mass wedding, Singapore
2 Couple outside church, Peru
3 Royal wedding, Indonesia
4 Jewish wedding, USA
5 Sikh wedding, England

The students discuss and describe a few of the weddings. This can be done in groups or as a class. They also discuss how these differ from weddings in their own country.

PRONUNCIATION

1a ○ ● **Explanation** Intonation is important in all languages and meaning often depends on where the stress falls in the sentence. Students need a lot of practice in sentence stress to help in communication.

● **Practice** Students work in pairs to work out the main stresses in the first eight lines of Suzi and Sylvia's conversation. Play that part of the tape for students to check their answers. Ask some of the pairs to read out the dialogue for the class, paying particular attention to stress and intonation. The rest of the class should listen and comment on mistakes.

A	**Sylvia**	Are you *ready*, Suzi?
	Suzi	No, I can't do this *dress* up . . . I must *hurry*, it's a quarter past *three*.
	Sylvia	It's too *small* for you.
	Suzi	No, it *isn't*. I'm on a *diet*, because when the NYT season finishes, I'm going to *America*.
	Sylvia	Keep *still*, Suzi. *Why* are you going to America?
	Suzi	To make that *film*. I got the *part*. Shooting begins next *month*.
	Sylvia	Suzi! That's *terrific*!

b ● Students work in pairs using the stressed words only, as prompts to recreate the dialogue. They need not worry about getting the dialogue exactly right.

2 ○ ● **Explanation** In this pronunciation exercise, students need to distinguish between similar vowel sounds. As they can see, spelling and pronunciation in English do not correlate! Students can use their dictionaries to check the pronunciation of the words. Then practise the pronunciation as a class.

○ ● **Practice** Students work with a partner to find the answers. Then read out the pairs of words so that the students can hear the differences and correct their answers.

A		
do/look **D**	flower/our **S**	jaguar/bag **S**
make/arrange **S**	pretty/city **S**	season/ready **D**
school/put **D**	want/front **D**	new/you **S**
champagne/rain **S**	wear/clear **D**	present/leave **D**
bouquet/quiet **D**	diet/lion **S**	yacht/crashed **D**

3 ○ ● **Explanation** Here is another example of how important intonation and stress are to meaning. The same words said differently convey completely different messages. Students have to link the pronunciation/intonation to the right picture.

○ ● **Practice** Students look at the pictures and try to imagine the situation for each. Discuss what might be happening in each picture. Play the cassette. Ask students to link each statement/question to the appropriate picture.

T.9.3	1 No *thanks*! (indignant, personal)
	2 No, thanks. (impersonal, in café)
	3 It's *gone*! (surprise, outrage)

4 It's gone. (railman to passenger)
5 How did *you* get there? (one tramp to another at Buckingham Palace)
6 How did you get *there*? (very surprised)

A	1e 2c 3d 4a 5b 6f

LISTENING

1 ○ ● **Explanation** This exercise serves to introduce vocabulary to do with sailing, needed for exercise **2**. It also introduces the theme for the next episode of the story.

○ ● **Practice** Read the list of words to ensure students get the pronunciation right. Words like *dinghies*, *yacht*, and *crew* often cause problems. Students should use their dictionaries to help them with meaning and pronunciation.

2 ○ ● **Explanation** This is a listening comprehension exercise.

○ ● **Practice** Students read the questions before you play the cassette so they know what to listen out for. Then play the cassette through once. Students can work in pairs to discuss and answer the questions. Play the cassette again for students to check their answers. Play it as many times as is needed, before checking the answers as a class.

T.9.4	**Max**	Toby, a word with you. Sylvia tells me you sail.
	Toby	I can sail, yes.
	Max	Big boats, or little dinghies?
	Toby	I've done some ocean racing.
	Max	Good. Would you like to crew for me? I've entered my boat *Lion* for the Fastnet Race.
	Toby	Would I like . . . I certainly would.
	Tom	The Fastnet? Hey, can I come?
	Max	You? Can you sail?
	Tom	You bet. I've sailed since I was a boy. My dad was a boat-builder. Big yachts, like yours.
	Max	Come and see me in Cowes on Sunday. Both of you.
	Suzi	The Fastnet? Isn't that the most dangerous race there is?
	Toby	Of course not? It's as safe as houses these days!

1 Max mainly, also Toby, Tom, and Suzi talk.
2 Max
3 A big (racing) yacht
4 An ocean race
5 Tom
6 Tom's father
7 An ocean race with yachts
8 dangerous (but Toby says it is safe these days)

○ ● **Practice**   Students can work in groups to do this exercise. Compare answers as a class and discuss the expressions you have in your language that are like these.

A

as cool as a cucumber	as old as the hills
as nice as pie	as tough as old boots
as dry as a bone	as good as gold
as sharp as a needle	as drunk as a lord
as white as a sheet	as clean as a whistle

Students can learn one or two of these expressions and find out where they can be used appropriately. For example, you can talk about a child being *as good as gold*, but not a piece of work, i.e. it refers only to behaviour.

Options 9

SOCIAL IDIOMS

○ ● **Explanation**   It is the correct use of idiomatic expressions that can confuse foreign learners. Here is practice in applying some simple expressions to the appropriate situation.

○ ● **Practice**   Read the idiomatic expressions with the right intonation and make sure students understand them. Students then work in pairs to link a situation or statement in **A** with an idiom in **B**.

A

1 k	5 d	9 n	13 j
2 m	6 a	10 e	14 p
3 c	7 i	11 f	15 g
4 o	8 b	12 h	16 l

LANGUAGE

○ ● **Explanation**   These expressions (similies) are used as comparisons in English. Most languages have similar expressions. Students match a part from **A** and a part from **B** to form the right expression. They may need to use an English-English dictionary to help them.

FURTHER PRACTICE

○ ● **Explanation**   This is an oral fluency exercise which focuses on the use of superlatives.

● **Practice**   Students should do the exercise in small groups so they can discuss their answers and then share them with the class. If some of the group have different ideas, those should be reported, too, e.g.

We all think Anna is the smartest person.
Some of us think that Max is the cleverest and some of us think Tom is.
. . . and . . . think Toby is the best-looking one. The rest of us think Poppy is the best-looking, etc.

ENRICHMENT

a/b○ ● **Explanation**   It is often difficult to know when to use *need*, *should*, *must*, or *have to*, especially when the difference between giving advice and telling a person to do something is slight. The choice of words is important so as not to give offence. If you were to put the words on a scale, it would probably look like this, but context and intonation often have an effect, too.

Advice   need to   should   have to   must   **Obligation**

←—————————————————————————————→

○ **Warm-up**   To introduce the idea of giving advice, discuss ways of giving advice in the students' own language.

● **Practice**   Students work in small groups or in pairs to discuss each of the situations. They choose one or more of the expressions listed to give each of the people advice.

A **Possible answers**

1 Why don't you complain about their noise?
   Have you considered sending them a rude letter?
   If I were you, I'd make an official complaint to the police.
2 If I were you, I'd use a ladder.
   Why don't you get the ladder?
3 If I were you, I'd go to a dentist.
   Why don't you go and see the dentist?
4 How about taking the car to the car wash?
   Have you thought about having your car repainted?
6 Perhaps you should ask someone to help you.
   Have you thought of hiring a removal company?
   Why don't you ask for help?

SMALL TALK

○ ● **Explanation**   This exercise practises the emphatic *do/does*, e.g. *It **does** look nice*, which emphasizes the comment much more than *It looks nice*.

● **Practice**   Students must match the statements they hear with the correct topic. Check their answers, then practise the intonation with them.

● **Extension**   Students in pairs can practise making general comments and giving compliments to each other, e.g. *I **do** like your earrings*.

T.9.5

A

1 What a lovely old church!
   Yes, it's beautiful. It's fourteenth century, I think.
   It may be beautiful, but it does feel cold!
2 Who did the flowers? Aren't they pretty?
   Yes, they do smell gorgeous.
3 Sssh. Here comes the bride.
   What a super dress. She's lovely.
   She does look radiant!
4 What's this hymn? I don't know it.
   Listen to the organ, you can hear the tune.
   It does sound sad. I like lively music at a wedding.
5 Have a piece of cake.
   Thank you. Mmm, it does taste good.

REVISION

○ ● **Explanation**   This is a mini-survey in which students ask questions about the topics listed in the three groups in order to find another student who agrees with them. It is an activity for the whole class and gives some revision of the present perfect. Students should study the example answers before starting the survey.

● **Practice**   Students should first of all tick the things they like in each section before they begin asking their questions. Then they interview (and are interviewed by) three different people and put a tick or a cross in the appropriate column.

● **Extension**   Students identify one of the other students who agrees with them on the most topics in each group. They then tell the class what the similarities are, e.g.

. . . agrees with me on several things. We both think that spicy food is best . . .

10
Preview

1 Passive

a ○ ● **Explanation** This unit introduces the passive voice. The difference between the active and passive is what happens to the subject of the sentence. In a passive sentence the object of the verb becomes the subject, either because it is more important or interesting than the subject, or because the subject is not known. In this exercise, students identify the passive form and the main difference between active and passive sentences.

○ ● **Practice** Students study the pictures and read the sentence that describes each one. The first picture shows that the subject, i.e. the person who stole the bicycle, is not known. The second picture illustrates a situation where the subject is less important, i.e. the speaker is more interested in the house than the painter.

Ask students to underline the verbs. Write the verbs on the board.

b ○ ● Students now look at the second pair of pictures. These identify the subjects and give them importance in an active sentence. Students compare the pictures and tense forms and try to identify the form and use of the passive voice. Ask questions to help the students' understanding, e.g.

Who has stolen the bicycle?
Who is painting the house?
In each picture what is more important to the speaker, the stolen bicycle or the thieves?/the house or the painter?

Students read the rules for the passive. Make sure they understand the use of the passive. Ask them if it is used in the same way in their own language.

c ○ ● Students identify the passive tenses. Read the sentences as a class. Let students work in pairs to underline the verbs and identify the tenses. They may need to be reminded that they are the same as active tenses. If it helps them, they may like to convert the passive sentences to active ones to check the verb form in order to identify the tense. Check the answers as a class.

A
1 is being redecorated (present continuous)
2 is going to be rewired (*going to* future)
3 will be painted (future simple)
4 were made (past simple)
5 have not been bought (present perfect)
6 were being painted (past continuous)

2 *have/get something done*

○ ● **Explanation** *Have/get*+object+past participle is a very useful expression in English. It is used to describe things we want other people, especially skilled people, to do for us, e.g. cut our hair, mend our car, build a swimming pool. It is a way of distinguishing between someone doing a job him/herself or a professional person doing it for him/her. It is sometimes called 'the causative'.

Note *Have* and *get* are interchangeable.

○ ● **Practice** Read the list of services we can pay someone else to do for us. Students identify which of those things Hattie needs to *have/get done* to improve her boat.

A
get the roof fixed
have the boat painted
get a loo put in
have the engine serviced
get the steering wheel mended

Discuss how this structure is expressed in the students' own language. Often in other languages a grammatical distinction is not made between *doing something* and *having something done*.

- **Extension** Ask the students to add to the list of possible services, e.g.

  get my car serviced
  get my computer fixed
  have my television/radio mended
  have the roof repaired
  get the shopping delivered

3 Order of adjectives

a/b ○● **Explanation** English has its own rules for the order of adjectives describing a noun which simply have to be learnt and practised.

- **Practice** Students work in pairs to find the answers and compare them with the rest of the class.

A	
1	a long, grey, cotton jacket
2	old, brown, leather shoes
3	a fantastic, huge, modern flat
4	a lovely, big, new, red car

4 Vocabulary

- ○ ● **Explanation** Students are introduced to the weather and sailing vocabulary needed for Episode 10. In this exercise they classify the words under the two headings.

- ○ ● **Practice** Read the list of words for students to hear the pronunciation. Students can work in pairs to divide the words according to the picture they think they belong to. They will need to use their dictionaries. Compare answers as a class.

  Note Some words may be seen as fitting into either category, e.g. *conditions* could be *weather conditions* or *conditions at sea*. If the students explain their reasons well, then that is fine, as long as they are clear about the meaning of the words.

A			
1	conditions	blow (v)	
	meteorological	gale	
	storm		
2	well-equipped	coastguard	skipper
	rescue helicopter	crew	race (n)
	mayday signal	yacht	sea
	warning	mast	sheet

Stormy Weather

T.10.1 In the previous unit, Max had asked Toby and Tom to crew for him on his boat *Lion* in the Fastnet ocean race. In this unit we learn that a dangerous storm is threatening the race. The scene opens at the TV studio where Sylvia works. The news director calls Sylvia and her colleague, Hal, into his office to tell them that the meteorological (met) office had contacted them about a severe gale building up in the Irish Sea. He wants them to go to Cowes from where they will be able to report on how the race is affected. In Cowes, they learn that the storm is moving very fast and will definitely hit the race, affecting the smaller boats worst of all. Sylvia is clearly very worried. The officer reassures Sylvia by telling her that Max is a very good skipper and *Lion* is a well-equipped yacht. However, he is concerned about *Lion*'s position which is likely to be in the centre of the storm.

While Sylvia is on the air reporting on the storm, a Mayday signal is received from *Lion* saying that their mast was broken by a giant wave and they are in real trouble.

Note Cowes is on the Isle of Wight, a small island off the southern coast of England.

The people in this episode

Hal is a colleague of Sylvia's. He knows absolutely nothing about ocean racing but is willing to work with Sylvia to cover the Fastnet Race when it is threatened by the storm.

Bob is the news director and Sylvia's boss. He is efficient but also sensitive. He recognizes that Sylvia is concerned about the storm but still offers her the job of reporting on it. He organizes getting them to Cowes via Portsmouth as quickly as possible.

Sylvia is by now well-established and respected in her job in television. She accepts the job of reporting on the race's progress through the storm despite her emotional involvement.

- **Warm-up** Look at the pictures. Ask:

  Who are the people?
  Where are they?
  What has happened?
  Why is Sylvia so concerned?

  Play the cassette. Stop after each section and ask students what has happened in each section.

Suggested check questions:

What does the news director tell Sylvia and Hal about?
Does Hal know anything about sailing?
Who has friends in the Fastnet?
What is the name of their yacht?
Do you remember who they are?
Who does the news director want to report on the race?
Where must they go and how will they get there?
Is Max a good captain?
Is Lion *a good yacht?*
Is Lion *in danger?*

Performance 10

COMPREHENSION

1 ○ ● **Explanation**   Students check their understanding of the story by choosing the correct answer. First of all, they should try to do the exercise without referring back to the story. Then they can look back and check their answers.

○ ● **Practice**   Students can work in small groups to do this exercise. Discuss the answers as a class.

A

 1 colleague
 2 because he's got bad news
 3 Hal is not very interested in the Fastnet.
 4 she is upset
 5 with Hal
 6 The boats are at Cowes.
 7 very dangerous
 8 be hit by the storm
 9 Sylvia is working.
10 Weather conditions near Fastnet are terrible.
11 Some boats are in danger.
12 They haven't found *Lion*.
13 *Lion* is in distress.
14 Sylvia doesn't know about it.
15 Fastnet is off England.

2 ○ ● **Practice**   Students work in pairs to match a beginning from **A** and an ending from **B** to form sentences. Discuss the answers as a class.

A

 1 I have just received a message from the weather bureau.
 2 I don't know much about sailing but I enjoy watching the boat races on the river.
 3 Sylvia, you are looking terribly pale.
 4 Would you like to report on what's happening?
 5 Somebody will meet you and take you to Cowes.
 6 The storm will hit the boats in a few hours.
 7 The waves will get bigger and bigger.
 8 Max is very good at sailing and his boat is very new.
 9 Somebody has murdered two old people.
10 Sylvia is going to tell you all about the storm.
11 Some of the small boats are in trouble.
12 A huge wave has just broken *Lion*'s mast.

● **Extension**   Ask students in pairs or groups to decide who says each of the statements in exercise **2**. Discuss the answers as a class.

A

    1 the news director
    2 Hal
  3–5 the news director
  6–8 one of the coastguards at Cowes
 9–10 the news reader
   11 Sylvia
   12 the coastguard officer at Cowes

PRACTICE

1 ○ ● **Explanation**   Students identify spelling and grammar mistakes and correct them.

○ ● **Practice**   Students read the passage alone first and then work in small groups to identify and correct the mistakes. They can then look back at the story to check vocabulary and spelling. Discuss the answers as a class.

A

Here is the latest news from the Fastnet Race. We *have* just had a flash from the met *office*. There *is* news of a severe *gale* which has *hit boats* taking *part* in the race. Our *reporter*, Sylvia Coleman, *says* that some *boats are* likely to be in the centre of the storm. *Coastguards* say that the *weather* in the *area around* Fastnet is *terrible*. Air-*sea rescue* helicopters are *flying* over the area, and some *boats* are in *distress*. *Waves* are 15 metres *high*. Now, over to Sylvia Coleman.

2 ○ ● **Explanation** This is a question-forming exercise. Students also revise reported questions.

○ ● **Practice** Read the reported questions as a class. Make sure students understand them, then they work in pairs to try to remember the question for each statement. Many of them are idiomatic and students may not remember the exact question. In this case they should make up a possible question and check in the story for the question afterwards. Does their alternative mean the same as the actual question? Discuss the answers as a class.

A
1 'Something up?'
2 'Are you OK?'
3 'Do you want to cover the story?'
4 'What does that mean?'
5 'Are those boats going to be OK?'
6 'Do you know where any of the yachts are?'
7 'Do you know someone out there?'
8 'What's happening?'

3 a ○ ● **Explanation** This exercise practises the use and forms of the tenses in the passive.

○ ● **Practice** Students study the schedule in small groups. They then read the sentences about each boat and identify the number of the boat. Compare answers as a class.

A
Boat 8 has just been started.
Boat 4 will be finished soon.
Boat 2 is going to be painted light blue.
Boat 1 is being painted.
Boat 3 can't be started because they're waiting for some special wood.
Boat 6 hasn't been sold yet.
Boat 5 was painted yellow yesterday.
Boat 7 was called Mary but will now be called St Mungo.

b ● Students work in pairs and take it in turns to ask and answer questions about the boats. They check answers as a class.

A
1 Boat 4.
2 Boats 4, 5, and 6 have already been painted.
3 Seven of the boats have been sold.
4 Yes.
5 Miss Jellicoe has bought the green boat.
6 Number 5, Miss Grey's boat, and number 6 have not yet been named.

c ● Students make up their own questions about the boats to ask a partner. Make sure the passive voice is included. Compare questions as a class.

4 ○ ● **Explanation** Students revise the comparative form.

● **Practice** Students work in pairs. Each person chooses two boats to compare without telling their partner which they are. They describe the boats by comparing their size, width, mast, length, colour, and equipment. The partner must then try to identify the two boats from the description. Students use the adjectives listed to help their comparisons.

5 a ○ ● **Explanation** This exercise practises the order of adjectives when describing people.

○ ● **Practice** Study the chart as a class and discuss the differences in the students' own language. Often in other languages, the adjectives are placed after the noun, so the same rules do not apply.

b ○ ● First, as a class, find as many adjectives as possible to describe each of the people in the picture, and put them up on the board. Then students in pairs or groups write a sentence for each person, taking care to put the adjectives in the correct order. Check as a class.

c ● Students work in pairs or small groups to describe the people in their family. If possible, students can bring a family photograph to the lesson and another student can try and identify the member of family being described, as in the example.

PRONUNCIATION

1 ○ ● **Explanation** Students identify the main stress in some words introduced in this unit, and practise their pronunciation.

● **Practice** Say the words aloud together first. Let students practise saying the words with the correct stress. Then they can work in pairs to mark each word. Alternatively, students in pairs mark the stress. Then read the words aloud to the students and they compare their answers. Finally, practise pronunciation as a class.

A		
experienced	well-equipped	gale warning
issue	meteorological	unfortunately
in distress	severe	manage
coastguard	within	ocean
imminent	difficulty	signal

2 ○ ● **Explanation** Students identify the /ɔː/, /ɜː/, /əʊ/, and /eɪ/ sounds in the list of words.

○ ● **Practice** Students work in pairs to sort the words into the appropriate columns. Check the answers as a class. If necessary, read the words aloud before they start the exercise.

A

/ɔː/	/ɜː/	/əʊ/	/eɪ/
warning	third	blown	arrange
storm	heard	ocean	gale
force	word	suppose	raging
north		over	racing
story		coast	Mayday
		boat	latest

3 ○ ● **Explanation** Students practise reading phonetic script. All the sentences come from the text so students can recognize them.

○ ● **Practice** As a class, work out each of the statements using the stress marks to help with the intonation. Remind students that there are a lot of weak forms.

A

1 'Something up?'
2 'You're as white as a sheet.'
3 'Are you OK?'
4 'Nothing's happened yet.'
5 'You're due on air in ten minutes.'
6 'Do you know someone out there?'

LISTENING

1 ○ ● **Explanation** Students listen to four interviews and find out what happened to the crew of *Lion*. They will not understand everything but assure them that this is not necessary to be able to work out what happened.

T.10.2

1

James Harris	Mrs Morton?
Mrs Morton	Yes?
James Harris	James Harris. I'm ringing from the Royal Racing Club, in Plymouth.
Mrs Morton	Is it about Toby?
James Harris	Your son? The one who was on *Lion*?
Mrs Morton	Yes.
James Harris	I'm afraid the news isn't very good. They've found a life-raft with three survivors from *Lion* – but not Toby.
Mrs Morton	Not Toby?
James Harris	No. The three people on the raft were Sally and John Beamish and Tom Kingsley.

2

Interviewer	Tom. Tom Kingsley, isn't it?
Tom	Yes, that's right.
Interviewer	What about the others on *Lion*? Do you know what's happened to your skipper, Max Jefferson?
Tom	No. He and Toby Morton were still on *Lion* when a huge wave swept the raft away. We couldn't get back to the yacht.
Interviewer	Were they injured?
Tom	I don't think so. *Lion* is damaged, though. We lost a mast, you see, when she capsized. But she rolled back, and she was afloat when we last saw her.

3

Radio	Casualty? We're bringing in two survivors from the yacht race.
Casualty	Bad injuries?
Radio	Difficult to say. Who's on duty? Dr Bingham?
Casualty	Yes.

4

BBC Reporter	BBC, Dr Bingham. There are two survivors from the Fastnet here, aren't there?
Dr Bingham	Yes.
BBC Reporter	Which yacht were they on?
Dr Bingham	I don't know.
BBC Reporter	Are they OK?
Dr Bingham	They'll be all right. One has a broken arm and they've both got heavy bruising.
BBC Reporter	Can we talk to them?
Dr Bingham	Certainly not. They are both under sedation. Now, if you'll excuse me.
BBC Reporter	Doctor, what are their names?
Dr Bingham	Names? Jefferson and Morton.
BBC Reporter	From *Lion*! Thank you!

● **Practice** Students work in groups to listen to the cassette. Each of the four interviews gives a little bit of information about what happened to *Lion*. Pause after each interview so that the students can make notes. Play the cassette as many times as necessary.

They then discuss in their group what they think happened to the boat and its crew. Compare explanations in class.

2 ○ ● **Explanation**   This is a descriptive writing exercise to be done in newspaper style, i.e. short and to the point, with use of the passive voice.

○ ● **Practice**   Students use the information from the interviews to write their newspaper article.

READING

○ ● **Explanation**   This is an intensive reading exercise on the tragic Fastnet race of 1979 in which many of the yachts were lost and fifteen people killed.

○ ● **Practice**   Students read through the information and form their own opinions as to why things went wrong. They should also decide what they think of
a) what the Secretary of the RORC had to say.
b) what the Labour MP says.
c) the weather forecast given by the British meteorological office.
Students discuss in groups and then compare opinions with the rest of the class.

Options 10

QUANTITIES

a ○ ● **Explanation**   Students learn and practise the use of idiomatic phrases to describe a large amount of something when the exact amount is unknown, or unimportant.

● **Practice**   Read the phrases and ask students for their own examples like the one given: *thousands and thousands of pounds*. For example:

tons and tons of rice
hundreds and hundreds of ants
dozens and dozens of volunteers
hours and hours of hard work
days and days of waiting
miles and miles of cars
gallons and gallons of milk

Then students fill in each gap with the appropriate phrase.

Note   Some of these expressions are based on the imperial system of measuring, not the metric, so it may be necessary to remind the students of the old units of measurements, e.g.

gallon – litre
ton – kilo
mile – kilometre

A   Mildred bought *gallons and gallons* of wine for her party and *tons and tons* of cheese. She washed *dozens and dozens* of wine glasses – she invited more than fifty guests. But *hundreds and hundreds* of people came to drink it and she didn't have enough glasses or cheese. She sent Peter to the shop. Peter walked *miles and miles* but didn't find the shop. 'I've walked for *hours and hours*,' he said when he came back. But there was silence. The wine bottles were empty, the cheese plate was empty, and the flat was empty. And he didn't see Mildred again for *days and days*.

b ○ ● Students work in pairs to describe the pictures. Compare answers as a class.

A   **Possible answers**
1 dozens and dozens of people/hours and hours of waiting
2 gallons and gallons of milk
3 hundreds and hundreds of cows
4 hundreds and hundreds/bags and bags of letters
5 miles and miles of sand/days and days of travelling
6 thousands and thousands of flies
7 dozens and dozens/rows and rows of trees
8 rows and rows of houses
9 tons and tons of bread
10 miles and miles of rope

VOCABULARY

○ ● **Explanation**   This exercise is to revise vocabulary from recent episodes of the story.

● **Practice**   Students work in pairs. First, student A reads out his/her list for student B to categorize; then student B reads out his/her list for student A to categorize. The students make two columns for their words as in their books. The students need to know the words in order to categorize them. If they are in doubt, they can use their dictionaries.

Pleasant		**Unpleasant**	
A list	**B** list	**A** list	**B** list
rescue	experienced	gale	storm
well-equipped	friend	rage	broken
safely	coastguard	hit	threaten
sunshine	bouquet	severe	warning
marriage	bride	difficulty	distress
honeymoon		waves	dangerous
			panic

Note The categories are entirely up to the student as long as the meanings are known, e.g. one student may consider *waves* to be something pleasant. However if the first student objects to the category a word has been put in, the second student has to explain why he/she chose it.

- **Extension** Students may continue this exercise with word lists of their own. Here they must give a reason why they consider each word to be pleasant/unpleasant.

SMALL TALK

a ○ ● **Explanation** This exercise gives students a few more common expressions used to introduce or ask for opinions.

- **Practice** Students read the news items and think about what comments they could make, using the phrases given wherever possible. Then in pairs they take turns in talking about the news and agreeing/disagreeing, e.g.

  A *'What do you think of these oil companies? They're always putting up the prices and still they claim that they're not making any profit!'*
  B *'I know, it's terrible.'*
  B *'I'm sorry to hear that the match between Leeds and Real Madrid was a draw, but I'm glad that it was a good-humoured match.'*
  A *'Yes. There's too much hooliganism these days.'*

b ○ ● Students work in pairs or groups to make small talk about current items of news. They can bring newspaper articles that interest them to class, or comment on what they remember from recent news. This should be a freer exercise than **a** with emphasis on fluency, not accuracy.

FURTHER PRACTICE

○ ● **Explanation** This is a vocabulary exercise on words to do with repairing, etc. It also gives students a further opportunity to practise the passive form.

○ ● **Warm-up** Read the words listed and make sure students understand them. In particular, concentrate on the slight differences in meaning between *repair* (to mend something that is broken, *renovate* (to make something like new again), *decorate* (to paint something), and *rebuild* (to build something again). Remind them or ask them how the passive is formed, and refer them to the example. They are asked to use only the present continuous passive and the future with *going to* passive.

○ ● **Practice** Students work in pairs to write about what is being done or going to be done to each of the houses. Compare answers as a class.

Possible answers
House 2 is going to be sold.
House 3 is going to be demolished and rebuilt.
House 4 is going to be sold.
The windows of house 5 are being renovated.
The wall of house 6 is being repaired.
House 7 is being painted and decorated.

Workbook Answers

Grammar & practice exercises

1

Positive	Negative
You've walked	haven't walked
He's walked	hasn't walked
She's walked	hasn't walked
We've walked	haven't walked
They've walked	haven't walked

Questions	Short answers
Have you been	you haven't
Has he been	he has
Has she been	she hasn't
Have we been	we haven't
Have they been	they have

2

come	got
dyed	met
put	sent
tried	spoken
included	been
seen	spent
slept	announced
taken	dropped
won	done
published	

3a Jane She has also scored a 50 and a 100.
Shape: circle
Tim But he has scored two 5s, a 25 and a 100.
Shape: triangle
Nick But he has scored three 50s and a 100.
Shape: rectangle
Sue She has also scored two 25s.
Shape: star

3b Jane No, she hasn't, she's scored 170 points.
Tim No, he hasn't, he's scored 135 points.
Nick No, he hasn't, he's scored 250 points.
Sue No, she hasn't, she's scored 105 points.

5

	Interview	At home	At work
Friendly	4	7	8
Formal	6	2	5
Unfriendly	9	3	1

1

2	request	8	request
3	spontaneous decision/request	9	promise
4	refusal	10	refusal
5	offer	11	offer
6	prediction	12	prediction
7	spontaneous decision		

2 Possible answers
1 It's going to fall.
2 They're going to fight/have a fight.
3 She's going to have a baby.
4 It's going to rain./There's going to be a storm.
5 He's going to jump into the swimming pool.
6 She's going to play the piano.

3a
2 light/lighter
3 warm/warmer
4 bad/worse
5 early/earlier
6 pretty/prettier
7 good/better
8 exciting/more exciting
9 beautiful/more beautiful
10 hot/hotter

3b Possible answers
1 beautiful/more beautiful 3 prettier
2 hot/hotter 4 good/better

5
1 A man and woman
2 Two
3 In a supermarket
4 Not very well (She doesn't know what he likes.)
5 Cheese
6 Voice making an announcement
7 They don't buy any cheese.

1
1 I've got to go now.
2 No, he hasn't.
3 We shouldn't go.
4 They've got to catch the bus in five minutes.
5 No, I don't (have to wear a shirt).
6 He should go to the dentist.

2 She has to: be fit/like people/like travelling/be away a lot/know about first aid/wear a uniform/look smart
She doesn't have to: live in London/be tall/be young/speak six languages/fly a plane

3
1 How long has your family lived here?
2 Is there a lot of land?
3 What are you going to do with it?
4 When did you have a civil war in this country?
5 What's wrong with the church?
6 What can I do with this place to make money?

4

1	for	4	for	7	for
2	since	5	since	8	for
3	for	6	since		

5 tired and cross: Ian
relaxed and friendly: Donald
cold and formal: Philip
fussy and pompous: Nick

1a

suddenly	happily
badly	gently
fast	tidily
well	dangerously
carefully	safely
angrily	beautifully
hard	early
straight	simply
easily	late
nicely	

1b 1 quick/quickly   4 angrily/angry
2 correct   5 correct
3 careful/carefully

2 2 You've told Max, haven't you?
3 You have to work hard at college, don't you?
4 He plays the clarinet well, doesn't he?
5 You failed your exam, didn't you?
6 She's going to be a lawyer, isn't she?
7 You've won a lot of races, haven't you?
8 She's got her track suit, hasn't she?
9 She has to get up early, doesn't she?
10 We should catch the first train, shouldn't we?

3 2 Rita wants to run in the 100 metres.
Her trainer wants her to run in the 200 metres.
3 Suzi wants to be an actress.
Her parents want her to go to university.
4 The government wants to raise taxes.
Voters want the government to lower taxes.
5 Sylvia doesn't want to apologize.
Sir Robert wants Sylvia to apologize.
6 Archie wants to keep the castle.
The bank manager wants Archie to sell the castle.
7 Toby wants to finish his work.
Poppy wants Toby to go to Merlock.

4 2 is rising   6 live   9 likes
3 leaves   7 forgets   10 sees
4 am living   8 am leaving/   11 is seeing
5 rises   am getting up

5 1 swimming   4 running
2 skiing   5 tennis
3 football

1 If Jack *takes* the cabbages, the dog *will eat* the rabbit. If Jack takes the *rabbit*, the dog *won't eat* the cabbages, because dogs don't like them. So, Jack takes the *rabbit* across and rows back.
Now, if he *takes* the dog across, and comes back for the *cabbages*, the *dog* and the rabbit *will be* on the bank together, and the dog *will eat the rabbit*.
So, if he takes the dog across, he *will* have to bring *the rabbit* back with him.
Now, he and the rabbit and the cabbages are on this bank. If he leaves the rabbit with the cabbages, *it will eat* them. But if he *takes the cabbages* across and leaves them on the other bank with the dog, they *will be* safe, because *the dog won't eat* them.

2 1 correct   4 yourself/yourselves
2 themselves/herself   5 ourself/himself
3 correct   6 myself/ourselves

3 2 If you open the gate, I'll drive through/I'll park the car.
3 If you buy the cheese, I'll post the letters.
4 If you peel the potatoes, I'll wash the lettuce.
5 If you run after him, I'll call the police.

4a Josie: computer programmer
Bill: fire-fighter

4b **Josie's job**
yes: interesting, long hours, earn a lot, work for yourself, sit at a desk
no: hard work, interesting people
Bill's job
yes: interesting, hard work, interesting people
no: long hours, earn a lot, work for yourself, sit at a desk

1 **Possible answers**
2 Could I have a cotton one, please?
3 I'd like the slimfit ones, please.
4 Can I try on the blue ones, please?
5 I'll take the leather one, please.
6 I'd like three glass ones, please.
7 Could I have a large one, please?
8 We'd like three small ones, please.

2 Defining: 2, 4, 5, 6, 8
Non-defining: 1, 3, 7

3a person: who/that
people: who/that
place: which/that/where
time: when
thing: which/that

3b 1 where   4 that/which   7 that/which
2 which   5 who/that   8 who/that
3 when   6 that/which

1 2 Eric asked if Sally had seen James today. Sally explained that she had only arrived five minutes ago.
3 Fay asked if Alistair was directing the play. James explained that Alistair was doing the auditions, but Diana would direct the play.
4 Sue asked if the Dixons would act together in this play. Frank explained that they wouldn't be in it. Donna Dixon was in America, and Peter had broken his leg last week.
5 Dave asked if Lucy was going to stay in a hotel. Lucy explained that it was much too expensive. She was staying with some friends near the station.

2

Sarah	Because I've been on night duty and I haven't had any sleep.
Mother	Do you like night duty?
Sarah	No, I don't.
Mother	Why not?
Sarah	Because I never see my friends.
Mother	Why don't you find a nine-to-five job?
Sarah	Night work pays very well, and I like nursing. I'll get more sleep next week, I promise.
Mother	I don't think you will.
Sarah	Can we have supper early? I want to watch a film on TV.
Mother	OK, but you should go to bed early.
Sarah	That isn't what weekends are for!

3a 1 When he rides a bike, he falls off.
2 When she oversleeps, she's late for work.
3 When Matthew goes climbing, he doesn't use a rope.
4 When Henry and Jane play tennis, Jane wins.

3b **Possible answers**
2 When there are flowers nearby, she sneezes.
3 When he reads, he falls asleep.
4 When he opens the window, the door slams.
5 When she sunbathes/lies in the sun, she get sunburnt.
6 When they watch sad films, they cry.

1 1 'd   5 had   9 goes
   2 'll   6 buy   10 would
   3 saw   7 'll   11 will
   4 'd   8 comes

2a harder/the hardest
   straighter/the straightest
   safer/the safest
   earlier/the earliest
   more beautiful/the most beautiful
   cleverer/the cleverest
   gentler/the gentlest
   happier/the happiest
   more peaceful/the most peaceful
   drier/the driest
   friendlier/the friendliest
   newer/the newest
   more dangerous/the most dangerous
   better/the best
   fuller/the fullest
   more horrible/the most horrible
   faster/the fastest
   tidier/the tidiest
   more excited/the most excited
   simpler/the simplest
   worse/the worst
   more comfortable/the most comfortable
   wetter /the wettest

2b 1 Mount Everest is the highest mountain in
     the world.
   2 Concorde is the fastest plane in the world.
   3 Diamonds are the hardest stones in the
     world.
   4 Brazil is the biggest country in Latin
     America.
   5 Which is the most expensive car in the
     world?
   6 Where is the longest river in the world?

3 3 does he?   7 wouldn't he?
   4 won't she?   8 will she?/she won't
   5 don't you?   9 would he?
   6 he wouldn't   10 they will

4 Sam

1

Positive	Negative
He was playing	He wasn't playing
They were going	They weren't going
I was shutting	I wasn't shutting
We were writing	We weren't writing
She was pulling	She wasn't pulling

Positive	Question
They were looking	Were they looking?
I was climbing	Was I climbing?
It was raining	Was it raining?
He was getting	Was he getting?
You were swimming	Were you swimming?
We were waiting	Were we waiting?

2 The sun was shining, and birds were singing
in the trees. The phone was ringing, the
radio was playing some music, and her
mother was standing at the door, saying,
'Get up'.

3 1 am   5 lands/won't know
   2 arrives   6 barks
   3 won't phone/gets   7 comes
   4 go   8 is

4 1 You must get up.
   2 You should go to the dentist.
   3 You should wear trousers./You should be
     wearing trousers.
   4 You must wear a hard hat here.
   5 You must wear trainers in the gym.

5a a 2   b 5   c 6   d 1   e 3   f 4

5b 1 c   2 b   3 f   4 e   5 d   6 a

1a floor/clean   speakers/replace
   heating/check   walls/paint
   lights/put in   windows/mend
   seating/repair

   Possible answers
   They are going to have the heating checked.
   They are going to have the lights put in.
   They are going to have the seating repaired.
   They are going to have the speakers
     replaced.
   They are going to have the walls painted.
   They are going to have the windows
     mended.

1b **Possible answers**
   The walls have been painted.
   The speakers have been replaced.
   The seating is being repaired.
   The heating is being checked.
   The windows are going to be mended.
   The floor is going to be cleaned.

2 **quality**: attractive, comfortable, expensive,
     horrible, valuable
   size: fat, high, huge, large, little
   age: middle-aged, modern, new, old
   colour: black, cream, green, grey, orange
   material: brick, glass, gold, metal, plastic

3 Sid said she wasn't, and asked why (Hal
   wanted her).
   Hal said there was a big story – there had
   been an earthquake in Italy. Sid said he
   would ring the newsroom. Hal said thanks
   (thanked him) and said he would be in the
   office. Sid said he'd send her there.
   He asked if that was the newsroom, and if
   Sylvia was there. He said that Hal was
   looking for her.
   Sylvia said hello to Sid and asked what was
   up. Sid said that Hal wanted her, and that he
   was waiting for her in the office.

4 1 Shannon, Irish Sea   3 Rockall
   2 Lundy   4 Fastnet

Workbook Tapescripts

UNIT 1   EXERCISE 5

T.1 1 **Woman** When are you going to write that letter?

Man I told you, when I've got time. I've got a meeting now.

2 **Man** Good afternoon. My name is George Wheeler, from Highlife Insurance. I've come about your car. We have to see it before we can pay.

Woman Yes, of course. This way, please. The car is in the garage.

3 **Father** Why did you put those books there?

Son Because I wanted to.

4 **Interviewer** That sounds great . . . And what did you do then?

Author Ah, then I went to America. I wanted to do some research for my second book.

5 **Woman** Are you working in here all day, Mr Jameson?

Man No, only this morning. The room will be free from 12.30.

6 **Reporter** Have you anything to say about the situation in China?

Politician No, I have nothing to say at this time. No decisions have been made yet.

7 **Wife** Is the map in the hall?

Husband I think so. Hang on, I'll go and see.

8 **Woman** Are we going to finish those plans, Alice?

Woman Yes, good idea. I'll bring them in at three o'clock.

9 **Reporter** Why have those buildings fallen down?

Politician I'm not answering that question.

UNIT 2   EXERCISE 5

T.2 **Man** They're over there, I think.

Woman Where?

Man On the right.

Woman Yes, of course. What kind do you like?

Man I don't mind.

Woman Well, how about English cheddar or French brie? Or there are some German and Austrian ones as well. And Dutch, of course.

Man Um, English ones, I think.

Woman Hard or soft?

Man Aren't English ones all hard?

Woman Oh, no.

Tannoy Customers, today we have reductions on the bread counter.

Man I don't like the blue sort. I think I'd prefer a hard one.

Woman Red, then? Or plain?

Man I don't mind, as long as it's not too strong.

Tannoy The store will close in ten minutes.

Woman We have to hurry. We need a lot of things.

Man Well, leave this. I don't really like it, you know.

Woman Why didn't you say so?

UNIT 3   EXERCISE 5

T.3 **Woman** Hello. My name's Jane Coulson. I work for English Heritage, and I'm visiting everybody in your village to discuss our plans for the castle. Are you Philip Gillette?

Man Yes, I am. Can I see your identification, please? Thank you. Now, what do you want to tell me, Miss Coulson?

Woman Hello. My name's Jane Coulson. I work for English Heritage, and I'm visiting everybody in your village to discuss our plans for the castle. Are you Ian Mackay?

Man Yes. Is it a questionnaire? I see. I'm afraid I'm very busy. I really haven't got time to stand here talking about the castle.

Woman Hello. My name's Jane Coulson. I work for English Heritage, and I'm visiting everybody in your village to discuss our plans for the castle. Are you Donald Harris?

Man Yes. Come in, you don't want to stand out there, it's cold this evening. How can I help?

Woman Hello. My name's Jane Coulson. I work for English Heritage, and I'm visiting everybody in your village to discuss our plans for the castle. Are you Nick Jolly?

Man Yes, I am. Please come in, I don't want to catch cold. No, don't put that on that table, it could mark it. You know, you should have made an appointment to see me.

UNIT 4   EXERCISE 5

T.4 1 **M** At the turn it's Robson for Canada, just ahead of Delardier from France; he's steaming through the water, it's going to be a close thing, now Burgholt from Sweden is catching up, this isn't his stroke, but my word, he's doing well . . .

2 **F** One point nine six seconds there, just behind Müller at this stage, conditions are bad now, they're getting worse all the time; we needed snow, but this is too much . . .

3 **M** Goal! It's a goal! Hazlitt has scored again. A hat-trick for Hazlitt!

4 **F** They're off. Yolande is the first to draw ahead, going smoothly. Then its Godfrey, Smithson, and Kennet in a bunch. Oh, Yolande has fallen – I think there was a spot of trouble there; Yolande is rolling on the ground, holding her leg. Now, they're coming to the end of the first lap, and it's . . .

5 **M** Volley, Davey hits it to the back of the court, Jenkins returns it with a backhand, skims it over the net, it's out . . . no, the umpire says in . . .

UNIT 5   EXERCISE 4

T.5 **Interviewer** What do you do, Josie?

Josie I'm a computer programmer.

Interviewer Who do you work for?

Josie I work for myself. I work at home.

Interviewer Is it hard work?

Josie No, it isn't hard, but I work long hours.

Interviewer Is it well paid?

Josie Yes, I earn a lot. But I have to spend money on training all the time.

Interviewer Why is that?

Josie In this business you have to keep up to date. There are always new developments, and new techniques to learn.

Interviewer Is it lonely work?

Josie I suppose so. You don't get to meet many people. But I like that. I'm not very sociable.

Interviewer So you enjoy your job?

Josie Yes, it can be very interesting.

Interviewer You're a fire-fighter, Bill.

Bill That's right.

Interviewer Is it hard work?

Bill Yes, I think so. It's difficult work, and it can be very dangerous.

Interviewer Do you earn a lot?

Bill Not really. We don't earn as much as the police. You earn more in business, insurance, things like that. But that's boring work. Being a fire-fighter is interesting. I meet interesting people, and I don't like sitting down. A desk job is terrible.

Interviewer Do you work long hours?

Bill Sometimes, yes. If there's an emergency, then we work until it's over. But normally, no, we don't work long hours. You can't; you have to be rested and fit to do this work. I like that, because it gives me time to be with my family and do some sport.

Interviewer Do you work overtime?

Bill Yes, sometimes. At holiday time, when people are away, you sometimes get to work overtime. But it's all controlled, the hours you can work, like I said.

UNIT 6   EXERCISE 4

T.6   She used to have short black hair and she always wore dark glasses. She used to wear very short skirts and high heels, and she used to carry a tiny bag.

Now she's got long fair hair and she wears plain glasses. She wears long skirts and flat shoes, and carries a big shoulder bag. She usually has a hat on. She never used to wear hats.

UNIT 7   EXERCISE 4

T.7   1a Which way is it?
         This way.
     b Go down past the office.
         This way?
     c Not that way, this way!
    2a Tea? Coffee?
     b What do you drink in the morning?
         Coffee.
     c This isn't tea! Ugh, it's coffee!
    3a And the prize is . . . a black jacket!
     b Have you got something plain? A black jacket?
     c What's she wearing?
         A black jacket.

4a Bring plenty of food, right?
 b That's the man who hit my car!
     Right!
 c I'll be there at six.
     Right.
5a That's six people.
     Oh, and Harry's coming.
 b Watch out, Harry's coming!
 c Did you say Harry's coming?

UNIT 8   EXERCISE 4

T.8   **Lucy** Have you ever seen a ghost?

Monica Yes, I think so. I was staying at an old hotel in Wales. It was late at night and I was on my way to bed. I looked up, and I saw a young man standing at the top of the stairs, looking down. He was wearing black trousers and a white shirt. He was holding a book in his right hand. He was tall and thin, and he looked ill. I thought he was looking at me and I was just about to say something when I heard a noise behind me. I turned around and saw a lovely young woman in a long dress. She was smiling at him. But when I turned to look at the young man again, he had gone, just vanished into thin air. I don't know where he went. Of course, the woman had disappeared when I looked again, so I think they must have been ghosts.

Lucy What about you, Sam, you've stayed at this hotel. Did you see anything strange?

Sam Well, I don't know if they were ghosts, but they do sound like the people that Monica saw. I was also on my way to bed, and when I was half-way up the stairs, I saw a man wearing dark trousers and a white shirt. He was walking down the stairs, smiling at somebody, or so I thought. He had a book in his hand. I remember that. I also turned round, and saw the beautiful young woman. But I don't think she was wearing a long dress. It looked more like a nightdress to me. Anyway, the same thing happened. When I turned to look at the man again, he was gone. It was very strange. I often think about them and wonder who they were.

 T.9   1 He's going to drop her, I know he is . . . What's her middle name? Morley? That's a funny name for a girl, I suppose it's her mother's family name, or . . .
         Ssssh!
    2 Happy birthday sung to Jennifer.
    3 . . . and I now pronounce you man and wife.
    4 As you know, Jessica comes from Scotland, and she's now going back to her native land. She's been with us for seven years, and I can truthfully say that everyone in the company will miss her.
    5 Man: Did you know him well?
         Woman: Oh, yes. We were great friends. It's so sad . . . but he had a good long life. He was 93, you know. Still, I'll miss him . . .
    6 I have the envelope here with the name of the winner of the best actor category. This is thrilling – who is it going to be? And the winner is . . . . . . Stanley Hopkins, for MacAdder in *The Day We Left*.

UNIT 10   EXERCISE 4

T.10   There are warnings of gales in sea areas Lundy, Fastnet, Irish Sea, Shannon, and Rockall.
Lundy, northerly severe gale force 9, decreasing to gale force 7.
Fastnet, north-westerly hurricane force 12 imminent.
Irish Sea, westerly severe storm force 11, soon.
Shannon, north-westerly severe gale force 9, increasing to storm force 10.
Rockall, easterly gale force 8, increasing to severe gale force 9 soon.

Word play

1 break, bridge, decide, environment, kneel, long, microphone, motorway, parent, pay, pretty, price, region, replace, rock, roundabout, single, steep, through, wrong.
Odd word out: Germany

2 bike fridge disappear band area sad

3 1 **Across** 1 post 5 envelope 7 book 8 fold
    Down 2 stamp 3 paper 4 type 6 label
  2 medicine: dose drugs aspirin medicine
    sport: athlete sport record
           test for race

4 **Across** herself rehearsal nervous lend
          pollution voice free blame time
          luck

Down development scream reason let
       normal ghost special

5 2 **Possible answers**
Friday: conservatory, flowers
Saturday: flowers, kiss, conservatory, back door, get engaged,
          engagement, wedding day, drop
Sunday: invitation, organize, witness, reception, engagement, couple
Monday: engagement, present, ring, filming, choose
Tuesday: wedding day, flowers, reception, honeymoon, kiss, witness,
          couple, ceremony

6 1 wave/engine   4 slim/severe   7 sail/yacht
   2 sink/upset   5 good-looking/alone   8 sail/crew
   3 serviced/dry-cleaned   6 weather/mast

Oxford University Press
Walton Street, Oxford OX2 6DP

Oxford New York Toronto Delhi Bombay
Calcutta Madras Karachi Petaling Jaya
Singapore Hong Kong Tokyo Nairobi
Dar es Salaam Cape Town Melbourne
Auckland

and associated companies in
Berlin Ibadan

OXFORD and OXFORD ENGLISH are trade marks of
Oxford University Press

ISBN 0 19 453453 9

Phototypeset by Wyvern Typesetting Ltd, Bristol, England

Printed in Great Britain